Museum of the

Unknown Writer

**Fiction by Eric Peterson**

*The Dining Car*

*Sunshine Chief*

*Life as a Sandwich*

# Museum
## of the
# Unknown
# Writer

### Essays

Eric Peterson

huckle
berry
house

Escondido, CA

Published by Huckleberry House
P.O. Box 460928, Escondido, California 92046
www.ericpetersonauthor.com

These essays first appeared in the daily online magazine *Pillar to Post*. Some of these essays appeared under different titles. In some instances, the essay content has been modified.

The author is indebted to *Pillar to Post's* founder and editor-in-chief, Thomas Shess.

Cover and interior design by Kathleen Wise
Editing, photo captions, and titles by Thomas Shess
Additional editing by Jennifer Silva Redmond and Katherine Brand
Cover photograph by Eric Peterson
Cover graphics by The Noun Project: Maxicons, Junichi Hayama

Museum of the Unknown Writer
First edition
Library of Congress Control Number: 2023901366

ISBN 978-1-7369834-3-0 (paperback)
ISBN 978-1-7369834-4-7 (ebook)
10 9 8 7 6 5 4 3 2 1
Printed in the United States of America

For my mother

And with thanks to Tom Shess

# Travelogue

# Eating Out

# Getting By

# Travelogue

The sleeper car Evelyn Henry and vista dome Warren R. Henry bring up the rear of Amtrak's Southwest Chief

## Private Varnish:
## A Birthday to Remember

Readers of my novel *The Dining Car* often tell me the book makes them want to take a long trip by train. Earlier this month, the stars aligned, and my wife, Teresa, and I took just such a trip—a chartered, one-of-a-kind journey I decided would commemorate my sixtieth birthday. Come, travel with us on two vintage private railroad cars, which industry insiders call *private varnish.*

### Wednesday, October 4

As with most of our cross-country train trips, this one originated at Los Angeles Union Station. To increase our odds of making the train, we traveled to Los Angeles the day before. We checked in to the Westin Bonaventure, a circular, vertically sprawling, contemporary hotel at 404 South Figueroa Street, in the heart of downtown. Our room on the twenty-eighth floor was clean and comfortable. I stood at the window in the late-afternoon sun, transfixed by the sweeping view of gridlock in every direction. It reminded me how lucky we were to be boarding a train.

It was here at the Bonaventure that Teresa and I met up with our three traveling companions: my brother, Chris, an avid reader on all things food and, in a past life, a trencherman of legendary proportions; Pat, an entertaining, quick-witted, long-standing friend who is a recovering attorney; and Pat's tall, prepossessing companion, Susan, who has made a name for herself as a Silicon Valley consumer research brain—and beauty.

*The Westin Bonaventure Hotel in Los Angeles*

I confess to being somewhat apprehensive about traveling with this particular crew. Their penchant for fine dining, storytelling, and laughter was surpassed only by their predilection for bottle waving, and I wondered if we could get through two nights and two days on a moving train without any broken bones.

It was worth the chance.

To begin, the Bonaventure has an award-winning steak house on the thirty-fifth floor. When was the last time you took an elevator up thirty-five floors to dinner?

LA Prime uses the Bonavista Lounge, a bar one floor down, as its cocktail lounge, so it was there that our party shifted into high gear. Drinking stout martinis in the snare of a corny revolving bar, being surrounded by tattooed sightseers in cargo shorts and baseball caps, paying inflated prices for cocktails—the surroundings were questionable but our time in the lounge passed quickly. An hour later we were seated at a comfortable table in LA Prime's dining room, which has equally panoramic views of downtown Los Angeles but doesn't turn like a cheap carnival ride. If we want the room to spin, we have a better answer: add more gin.

We put LA Prime's kitchen through its paces. We started with the escargot in shell, of course, pairing the buttery snails with the loudmouth of a chardonnay that Teresa had been drinking in the bar. An order of the classic oysters Rockefeller gave Chris an excuse to call for two bottles of a light-bodied pinot grigio. In time we moved on to Caesar and wedge salads, both safe bets in a primo chophouse.

The crispy, roasted brussels sprouts didn't disappoint, and the au gratin potatoes were satisfactorily cheesy and

creamy. For the main entrée, Teresa, Pat, and Chris opted
for the prime beef—the various cuts of steak, perfectly
cooked, came out sizzling. Susan ordered the Chilean sea
bass. I opted for the free-range, grilled Colorado double-cut
lamb chops. The bold cabernet—inky, black cherry, with
a hint of vanilla—flowed. It was a wonderful, gleeful
kickoff dinner.

### Thursday, October 5

The next day at 5:00 p.m., traveling in a taxi van bursting
at the seams with luggage, we arrived at Los Angeles Union
Station. When they announced our train, we left the grand
waiting room, entered the main tunnel, and negotiated a
throng of commuters, my black roller bag doing the work
of a deliveryman's hand truck. Perched atop my suitcase
was a case of wine, the bottles hand selected a few hours
earlier from the tastefully stocked shelves of a fine-wine
shop within walking distance of our hotel.

I confidently led our band of travelers up the ramp
to Track 12, where Amtrak's Southwest Chief was slated
to board. We found the track empty. An affable, bearded
Amtrak agent in a golf cart spotted us lingering like lost
souls on the station platform near the track's terminus.
Hearing that we were traveling "private," he tried sending
us forward. "The private sleepers are all at the head-end
of the train," he said. "Back here is coach."

I explained our accommodations in more detail.
His face lit up.

"Oh," he said. "Then, you're definitely in the right place!"

Ten minutes later the Southwest Chief backed down
the tracks. On the rear of the train were two classic private

*The lower lounge of the* Warren R. Henry

railroad cars: the dome-lounge *Warren R. Henry* and
the sleeper car *Evelyn Henry.* A knowing eye would peg
their beige-and-navy-blue paint scheme as that of the
now-defunct American Orient Express. These clean,
stunning, '50s-era railroad cars would serve as our hotel
until we reached Chicago.

We mounted the open platform of the vista dome car
and entered the lower lounge. It was like stepping into a
tycoon's study: mahogany paneling, plush blue carpeting
with bold patterns, wine-colored sofas and lemon chiffon
barrel chairs grouped in inviting seating arrangements.

A solidly built trainman sporting Amtrak credentials
boarded behind us. He was the locomotive engineer, hoping
for a souvenir wine glass to replace one from a previous
trip that had broken. Jeff, the *Warren R. Henry's* talented,
low-key executive chef (he wears chef's whites), graciously
acceded to the engineer's request.

For this trip, in addition to Chef Jeff, our two private railroad cars came staffed with Kashleigh, the onboard service manager. Kashleigh quickly spotted a man on the open platform looking for his seat on the Amtrak train. Lithe, well-spoken, and tactful, she deftly steered the interloper to general boarding. Kashleigh could easily have passed for Halle Berry. Her sense of humor was as natural as her sense of service.

Teresa and I made our way through the vista dome car, past the elegant, formal dining room, to the *Evelyn Henry*,

*Heading to our suite via the narrow corridor of the* Evelyn Henry

where we found our assigned stateroom, the Grand Canyon Suite. This master suite had a queen-sized bed, double closets, and a full bath. We hurriedly dressed for dinner and returned to the lower lounge in time to watch our 6:10 p.m. departure from the open platform. The hazy Los Angeles sky was tinted fire engine red. We stayed on the open platform until the train's speed—and the dusty, swirling winds—drove us indoors.

By the time our train turned east toward Riverside, our party had settled upstairs in the sumptuous vista dome lounge, which is topped by curving panes of glass that afford 360-degree views. Kashleigh poured out crystal flutes

*The sumptuous vista dome lounge, upstairs in the* Warren R. Henry

of champagne from a 750 ml bottle of Moët & Chandon Imperial Brut.

Jeff came up the stairs and set out a plate of crab crescent cups to accompany a cheese platter and crackers with a spinach-artichoke dip.

This was how our trip began—basking in the exalted luxury of a bygone era, sipping champagne, watching twilight fall over the shantytowns, industrial yards, and suburban sprawl that constitute the heart of the City of Angels.

On curved sections of track, our observation post high above the *Warren R. Henry* gave us an unobstructed view of the train to which we were coupled: six double-deck Superliner cars, a baggage car, and two chugging locomotives.

Rising dead ahead, glowing gloriously orange, was a full harvest moon.

We ate dinner two hours later in the comfortable uphol-stered leather booths of the vista dome lounge. The tables were draped in starched linen. Each place was set with fine china and Waterford crystal. Jeff's ample cuts of filet mignon roast were topped with a creamy chanterelle mushroom sauce, accompanied by tarragon green beans and baked potatoes in miniature. A Wabash pumpkin cream pie, served in mini-pumpkins, was dessert.

After dinner, at Kashleigh's suggestion, we went to the open platform and sat on folding chairs under heavy woolen blankets, gazing hypnotically at the receding track, savoring our meal. Pat sipped Jack Daniel's from a solo cup. A startling number of freight trains passed us in the opposite direction, the cabs of their locomotives dark as death. We all

saw Barstow, at 9:51 p.m., but soon after that our heroic
travelers began peeling off for bed. Pat and I were sorely
tempted to remain on the open platform until Needles, at
12:18 a.m., but good sense prevailed. We retired in favor
of an early wake-up call when we'd have daylight again.

Sleeping aboard the train was like sleeping on a
platform wedged between the branches of a tree that's
being buffeted by a fierce storm. You have the sense that
there is little other than air beneath your bed. The howling,
swirling winds shift in direction and change in velocity.
So it went through the night. According to the speedometers
in the *Warren R. Henry*, the Chief often surpassed speeds
of ninety miles an hour. I had a fitful night, worrying that
the constant motion might be keeping Teresa awake. I was
wrong. She slept just fine.

### Friday, October 6

I awoke in the darkened stateroom at 5:35 a.m., keenly
aware that our train had stopped. Eager to greet the day,
I left our warm bed, gathered my clothes, and dressed in
the brightly lit bathroom. Latching the stateroom door
behind me with a soft click, I made my way down the
sleeper car's narrow corridor. I crossed the vestibule to the
*Warren R. Henry*, where for a few minutes I had the vista
dome lounge—and a dramatic desert sunrise—to myself.
Checking the timetable, I learned that the stop that had
awakened me was Winslow, Arizona.

Rats, I thought. I wanted to see that.

The Southwest Chief pressed relentlessly east. The sun
climbed, the morning brightened, and our family of cheery
voyagers gathered topside in our familiar buffalo wallow.

*Sunrise over the high desert east of Winslow, AZ*

Kashleigh kept our coffee mugs filled. Sometime after
Gallup, New Mexico, she served a signature breakfast from
Jeff's kitchen: Fred Harvey French toast; eggs to order;
supersized breakfast sausages sliced into manageable bites.

*A signature Bloody Mary pairs with the view from
the* Warren R. Henry's *vista dome lounge*

Jeff's Bloody Marys were garnished with chorizo
sausage and celery stalks. Affixed to this critical substruc-
ture, impaled on picks, were green olives, slices of lime,
gherkins, cheese wedges, jumbo shrimp, and filet-of-beef
burgers the size of chestnuts. An accompanying slice of
bacon stood shoulder deep in each glass, casting big brown
eyes at its flamboyant chorizo neighbor.

*The author and his wife, Teresa, on the station platform
at Albuquerque*

Our midday stop at Albuquerque lasted nearly thirty
minutes—enough time to disembark the *Warren R. Henry*
and stretch our legs. Teresa and I hoped for the good luck
of finding our daughter Katie and son-in-law, Lucas, waiting
for us on the station platform, but there was no sign of them.
They live in Albuquerque. Ahead of us, Amtrak passengers
streamed from the Superliner cars. We walked the length of
the train, falling in with our fellow travelers, many of whom
looked sleep deprived and regretful. It made us wonder how
different their trip was from ours.

Albuquerque sits at an elevation of 5,312 feet. The sky
was blue and the sun was hot. Against a stucco wall, a
line of Native American women sat at card tables, selling
jewelry. We'd seen these same women—and their same
wares—while staying at La Fonda on the Plaza in Santa Fe.
Susan surveyed the merchandise but didn't buy. We took
advantage of the extended stop to snap pictures—Chris and

Pat standing before the lead locomotive, the obligatory shot of me standing woodenly at the door of the Amtrak dining car, all of us assembled on the *Warren R. Henry's* open platform, waving.

As you might guess, our two private railroad cars drew a steady line of gawkers. Sadly, we never saw Katie or Lucas, but we couldn't say we were surprised. Both work pressing jobs—Katie as an English teacher at Albuquerque's Bosque School, and Lucas as an Air Force dentist. We knew it was a long shot that either one could get away to meet our train in the middle of a workday.

We left Albuquerque shortly after noon. Going east, the tracks skirt the dense cottonwood forests of the Rio Grande Valley, where Katie's Bosque School is located. It was here that I felt a pang of melancholy. I imagined that Katie might've heard the sound of the air horn on our passing train as she was delivering an English lesson.

On the stretch of track between Lamy, New Mexico, and La Junta, Colorado, the BNSF Railway has discontinued freight service. Instead, they use the Southern Transcon railroad corridor, which goes south of Albuquerque and bypasses the steep grades of Raton Pass. But through a combination of political arm twisting, state funding, and federal transportation grants, Amtrak has stuck doggedly with the original, historic route of Santa Fe's Super Chief, paying the track's maintenance expenses. This was considerably to our benefit. Our train went much slower on this single track that meandered through rugged, rocky terrain. The creeks and streams, the trestles and bridges, the ranches and tree-lined pastures—it made for ideal watching from the open platform.

*Lobster roll, tater tots, and pickle spear elegantly served on vintage fine china*

We were admiring the protected lands of the Santa Fe National Forest when we were called to lunch: cream of asparagus soup, lobster rolls, tater tots, and pickle spears. I can tell you from experience that the perfect wine pairing for tater tots and a lobster roll is PlumpJack Chardonnay, though Pat and Susan seemed partial to Pabst Blue Ribbon beer.

After lunch, Jeff found the Cleveland Indians game on the in-motion satellite TV for Teresa and Pat—both big fans. They watched the big-screen TV from the plush sofas of the lower lounge. Baseball was no match for the scenery, as far as Chris and I were concerned. We went out to the open platform, where the sun was warm on our faces. Susan soon joined us. She took a lot of pictures in panorama mode. There was a section of track where the previous day's eastbound Chief had struck a boulder and derailed, making the train twenty hours late. The damaged locomotive was still there, parked on a siding. As our train crept past the accident site, we got big smiles and a number of happy waves from the track-repair crew on the ground.

At Las Vegas, New Mexico, we passed the westbound Southwest Chief. It seemed a significant milestone in our trip, though I can't articulate precisely why. I also can't say why I found it so fascinating watching all those signal lights turn from green to red as we crossed their purview. Signal block after signal block, day or night, the sight of the changing lights pleased me immensely.

Late in the afternoon, I returned to our stateroom in the *Evelyn Henry*, showered, and dressed for dinner. Kashleigh served drinks in the vista dome lounge. Stops at Raton, New Mexico, and Trinidad, Colorado, were mere distractions to our cocktail party, which raged in the dome. I recall dramatic mountain scenery, several long tunnels, and at least two very dry gin martinis.

Dinner that night was served in the *Warren R. Henry's* formal dining room. Jeff's stuffed crouton Caesar salad and Copper River salmon with butternut squash risotto hit on all cylinders.

I had a moment of panic when Chris waved a freshly opened bottle of an expensive California pinot noir in the general direction of Teresa's nearly empty wine glass, insisting on filling it to the brim. My terror was for Chris's

*Chris at the dining table, eagerly awaiting dinner*

notoriously poor aim and the *Warren R. Henry's* pristine white tablecloth, but I'm happy to report that like Larry Bird ham-handing a three-pointer at the buzzer, Chris hit nothing but net.

### Saturday, October 7

I was up well before our scheduled 7:24 a.m. stop in Kansas City, where tragically Chris was detraining to catch a flight back to Reno for a previously scheduled engagement. The skies were gloomy. Streaks of rain dappled the glass of our vista dome. Kashleigh brought coffee. The mood in the lounge grew bittersweet as we all realized our grand adventure was coming to an end.

Approaching the Kansas City yard, our train negotiated the labyrinth of tracks with hesitance, as though, like the rest of us, it wasn't yet ready to drop Chris from the passenger manifest. Through sheets of rain beating down on the glass, the downtown high-rises got bigger. And then, at the bright red neon sign heralding Kansas City Union Station, we came to a stop. Jeff put several plastic bags of trash off the train. Our goodbyes with Chris were necessarily brief. We left him standing with his duffel bag in the drizzle alongside the *Warren R. Henry.* As the station disappeared from view, Chris had his back to us; he was helping a maintenance worker load our trash bags into a waiting Taylor-Dunn burden carrier.

From there, time seemed to speed up. Kashleigh served a breakfast of bacon and eggs. Pat and I petitioned Jeff for Bloody Marys—Jeff brought them with chasers of Coors beer. At Fort Madison, Iowa, braving the rain and cold, Pat and I stood on the open platform as we crossed the Mississippi River. Traces of locomotive exhaust swirled through the open platform, mingling with the scents of fresh river water and rain.

The Chief was pulling out of Mendota, Illinois, at 1:19 p.m. when Kashleigh served our final meal: beef and bacon sliders with french fries. We ate in the vista dome. The skies remained ominous. After lunch, Teresa and I took turns in our suite on the *Evelyn Henry,* packing our bags.

At 2:42 p.m., the four of us watched our last stop, Naperville, Illinois, from our accustomed swivel chairs in the vista dome. Downstairs, in the lower lounge, our small mountain of luggage was staged for departure. Though we knew it was coming, our arrival in Chicago seemed abrupt. One minute we were traversing the wide expanse of a railroad yard in broad daylight, admiring the dramatic city skyline, and the next we were surrounded by concrete pillars and shadow. Inching along, our train entered an underground world of perpetual twilight and came to a stop.

Rolling our suitcases down the long station platform, we made our way past the now-empty Superliner cars and the triumphant, idling locomotives. We entered Chicago's Union Station through double-glass doors and took an escalator up to the street, where we found ourselves standing on a busy Chicago boulevard in the rain. We flagged down a taxi.

"The Four Seasons Hotel, on East Delaware," I told the cab driver.

I have learned that returning to the real world after two days on a train is much like deep-sea diving. If you do it too quickly, it can come as a fatal shock to your system.

Passing through Brownwood, TX

## Summer Road Trip:
## Texas in the Rearview Mirror

Let's just say one of us overestimated how many AllSaints dresses, Madewell sweaters, and pairs of Levi's jeans, ASICS running shoes, and Lucchese boots would fit into a rented Lincoln Navigator—that is, after the flat-screen TV, computer monitor, bedding, and framed horse pictures had already been loaded.

The happy result? I'd have company on my road trip.

It was Memorial Day Weekend, and my daughter Caroline was relocating from Austin, Texas, to San Francisco. The obvious solution to our dilemma was that Caroline would follow me, her father, in a second, equally jam-packed SUV.

Four days on the road with my precious twenty-six-year-old daughter. Heaven. But the prospect of embarking on a road trip always engenders a certain amount of apprehension. I'm convinced it's in our genetic makeup— residual atoms from ancestral pioneers who crossed the untamed West in covered wagons. Caroline and I would be spared the perils of prairie fires and marauding Indians, but traveling through four western states we faced savagery of a different sort: gas station restrooms, two- and three-star low-rise hotels, and a plethora of casual-dining restaurants.

On our last night in Austin, leery of meals to come,
I steeled myself with a pork chop from Perry's Steakhouse
& Grille. Thick as a Henry James novel, with three ribs
protruding from the top of the chop and a slice of tenderloin
they call the *eyelash* served on the side, a pork chop at Perry's
will have you raising your hands and singing hosanna. This
moist, buttery, decadently fatty interpretation of "the other
white meat"—each bite loaded with notes of smoke and
bacon—is Perry's signature entrée for good reason.

The highways of Texas are a joy to travel. The smooth,
spit-shined asphalt surfaces put California's potholed
freeways to shame. The posted speed limits of seventy-five
miles an hour mean you can safely cruise at eighty, and my
Lincoln Navigator was up to the task. Its acceleration was
impressive, its air conditioning robust.

The soft leather appointments of the cabin enveloped
me in a cocoon of quiet luxury, and the Sirius satellite radio
served up a seamless selection of uplifting country music.
Passing trucks, I relished seeing the Navigator's LED turn
signals as they flashed on the side mirrors—like a police
cruiser.

For the record, the '80s-era Lincoln Town Car still
stands today as the best road-trip automobile ever made.
Nothing facilitated a weekend screamer like tooling around
in a big, stinkin', four-door rented Lincoln—some of those
weekends are among the better memories of my early adult-
hood, but mention Phoenix, Arizona, to me and I will deny
ever having set foot in the place. Mention it twice and my
lawyers will sue you for libel.

By the time Caroline and I reached Lubbock, Texas,
night had fallen. Exhausted and hungry, we checked in

to the Hilton Garden Inn. For spaciousness, comfort, and cleanliness, our rooms at this hotel rivaled any of their big-city, high-rise cousins. The hotel's glittering lobby was stunning, and the staff of leggy, impeccably tailored Lone-Star brunettes who welcomed us—well, in my next life I hope to come back a Texan.

We settled for a late dinner at a nearby sports bar. The bright overhead lighting, the banks of buzzing TVs, the multicolored menus with their pages stiff and glossy as children's storybooks, the bar tops tacky as glue traps— it was like eating in a nursery school. The chicken piccata came out defrosted, microwaved, and solidly breaded.

Even the garden salad tasted like Chicken McNuggets.

The next day, we caught Highway 40, a route that parallels nearly 1,000 miles of the BNSF Railway's Southern Transcon, one of the busiest rail corridors in the United States. Mile-long freight trains came in scores, gifts from a munificent God.

*Mile-long freight trains came in scores*

*Local Albuquerque flavor along historic Route 66*

In Albuquerque we met Caroline's sister, Katie, and Katie's husband, Lucas, for dinner at Ruth's Chris Steak House. Both girls ate sensibly. I, on the other hand, flouted cirrhosis of the liver and coronary artery disease by matching Lucas in a wild carnival of gluttony: a slew of Manhattans followed by too much red wine, calamari with spicy Asian chili sauce, a bone-in New York strip, and a fully loaded baked potato. Did I mention that I love my son-in-law? That night I slept well, certain I could make San Francisco by living off my body fat.

Monday was a long day of driving for Caroline and me—ten hours. By the time we made Flagstaff, I was desperate for lunch. Caroline found an elegant workaround to fast-casual dining: she led us to a Whole Foods Market, where I soothed the jackhammering in my head with a 750 ml bottle of San Pellegrino sparkling mineral water and two slices of a thin-crust vegetarian pizza from the store's impressive prepared foods section. We ate outside at a picnic table with a view of the mountains. The air was scented with pine.

On the last morning of our trip, leaving Barstow, California, passing through the Mojave Desert, I suffered a shock: it seemed Southern California was being overrun by an army of colossal robots from outer space. On closer inspection, these gargantuan beings were horizontal-axis wind turbines, arranged in hideous Orwellian eyesores euphemistically called "wind farms." I am convinced these blots on Mother Nature's splendor will be the bane of our generation. And as far as I could tell, only about one in ten was turning. What's with that? And who will dismantle these monstrosities when mankind comes to its senses?

*Driving through the Mojave Desert*

Like most road trips, this one ended too soon. Crossing the newish Bay Bridge into San Francisco, I panicked as I realized I'd have to return my Lincoln Navigator to the car attendants at AVIS. I'd become attached to this big black truck the way a cowboy ranging over four states might grow fond of his horse, and now I had to shoot it.

Caroline and I finished our trip on a high note—dinner at Tadich Grill, San Francisco's oldest restaurant, that landmark spot in the Financial District where my father and grandfather once dined. I had successfully delivered Caroline home—home to the site of her first job out of college, home to that bone-chilling summer fog, home to that bustling, Bohemian, disgraceful City by the Bay.

At our table near Tadich's busy kitchen, I mopped my melancholy with chunks of garlic toast dipped in the simmering tomato sauce of a seafood cioppino, knowing that our father-daughter road trip was one for the ages, thinking that in an era of flying, self-piloted cars, when cancer and heart disease are cured by a simple pill, when a technology called Hyperloop is moving people from place to place at 4,000 miles an hour, Caroline can tell her grandchildren that she once drove from Texas to California with her old man. In those days, she'll tell them, you had to stay awake and steer your own car, which traveled strictly on the ground. The journey took four grueling days.

*Tadich Grill—a San Francisco institution*

The sun sets and the fun begins

## Foodie Fun in a Motorhome

If you're anything like me, you spot a glitzy private bus, big as a Greyhound, tooling down the interstate, and you wonder who might be in it—what rock band, what country singer, what up-and-coming tour golfer?

You may be surprised to learn that most of these flashy, garish buses are owned by ordinary folks. I know this because my wife, Teresa, and I joined this particular club of itinerant travelers a few years back when we bought Sarah Palin's tour bus.

Yes, that Sarah Palin.

The Alaska plates were still affixed to this jet-black, 42' bus with a triple-slide floor plan, a tag axle, and the biggest Caterpillar diesel engine Country Coach has ever put in a motorhome. But other than a *Drill Baby Drill* bumper sticker Teresa found tucked away in an overhead cabinet, there was little evidence that this bus had once served as home away from home—and rolling campaign headquarters—to a former governor, vice presidential candidate, and lightning rod for modern presidential politics.

"Like owning Napoleon's horse," one wag quipped.

We bought the massive coach because I had a new novel coming out, and I convinced Teresa that I desperately needed it for book signings. I may be an unknown author, but what reader could resist taking a walk through Sarah Palin's tour bus?

These rigs are built for prolonged stretches on the road. Their legions of complex systems work to deliver the creature comforts of home: water, electricity, heat, air conditioning, and satellite TV. Our Country Coach has a full kitchen, a spacious master bedroom, a washer and dryer, an art niche and hutch, and an Italian etched-glass shower enclosure in the bathroom. The Onan 12.5-kilowatt diesel generator ensures that Teresa's hairdryer will function without limitation on any given day.

*Home on wheels*

People often ask me about life on the road. My answer is always the same. It's a fun, flexible way to travel. No hotels, restaurants only when you want them, and none of the hassle of airline travel and rental cars. I enjoy the serenity of driving. Teresa likes to cook. We can both work from the road, and once we're safely off the highway and parked for the night, we can toast our progress—and our new scenery—with a cocktail and a bottle of wine in the comfort of our own living room.

When not traveling for our own entertainment, or when not making appearances with the bus at book club meetings, where we flatten neighbors' shrubbery, crush curbs, and knock over trees, Teresa and I keep our Country Coach parked in an industrial building on the US-Mexico border. The cavernous space is climate controlled and fully secure. Our Country Coach is one of perhaps 150 similarly sized, jaw-dropping buses kept in the facility, called the Big Toy Depot. The crackerjack staff monitors air, power, and water levels on the coaches, coordinates maintenance, and even washes the rigs when they're delivered back to the barn. Like a marina, the Big Toy Depot charges its tenants by the foot.

*At the Big Toy Depot in Otay Mesa, CA*

## Thursday, January 25

Teresa and I were on our way to Otay Mesa to pick up our
Country Coach for a four-day trip when my brother, Chris,
called. He and his wife, Carla, own a big luxury coach, too—
a 43′ Monaco Diplomat—and together we were meeting
two couples in Borrego Springs, California, at a favorite RV
park. Chris had bad news. His house batteries were dead.
A mechanic was standing by to install replacements, but it
meant pushing our departure to late afternoon.

The business with the batteries, a stop for fuel,
gridlock getting out of San Diego at rush hour, an accident
that forced a one-hour freeway closure on I-15 at Pala Mesa,
and suddenly the all-knowing Garmin had us arriving in
Borrego Springs at 9:45 p.m. So it goes. It wasn't like we
had a plane to catch.

At the RV park in Borrego Springs, our friends John
and Debbie graciously held dinner for our late-night arrival.
They had recently bought a new motorhome—a dazzling
45′ Essex luxury motor coach by Newmar that dwarfs ours.
As we filed in to their stylish, tastefully appointed living
room, John and Debbie passed us big goblets of red wine
as anti-road-buzz medication. They introduced us to their
good friends Robert and Sandy, who travel in a brand of
coach that's the envy of all RVers: a stunning two-level,
steel and glass Prevost bus.

Pappardelle noodles, a red meat sauce, and garlic
French bread never tasted so good. Sandy made a fresh
green salad. The four couples clicked. We went through
eight bottles of wine. Robert's Hispanic ancestors, we
learned, once owned New Mexico from Las Cruces
to Deming.

**Friday, January 26**

The next morning, six of us gathered in the campground and walked up to Borrego's Christmas Circle, a town square with a round shape where music played over loudspeakers under tall pine trees, and where a low-key farmers market was underway. The day was already hot. Collectively we came away with four avocados, one dress, several tins of hummus, and two fresh-baked pies. Chris gave a few dollars to a weather-beaten woman who sat off to the side in a plastic chair. She wore a white nurse's costume and was collecting money to fight cancer.

The ensuing afternoon passed quickly. I tinkered with a circuit breaker panel, trying to figure out why our coach wasn't getting hot water. Teresa and I tow a Jeep Grand Cherokee behind our bus. I used the Jeep to drive Chris, Carla, and Teresa to the local grocery store, where we bought $400 worth of food, wine, and spirits. Our same cancer fundraising nurse was in the checkout lane ahead of us, buying Cheez-It crackers and wine. Chris wondered if he'd been scammed.

As twilight fell, Teresa went for a shower in the Country Coach and got nothing but cold water. Luckily for both of us, this RV park had showers in its attractive, Santa Fe-style pool complex. The showers were clean and hot, but the night air was chilly as we walked back to our coach. The party began in earnest next door in Chris and Carla's Monaco. Robert brought appetizers: beef short ribs that he'd smoked on his new Traeger grill. Chris poured vodka Rickeys and cooked eight humongous double-cut rib eye steaks on his own grill. My one vodka turned into three. Teresa contributed a colorful vegetable tian to the dinner.

It was a good party. Dancing after the late meal, one of the ladies took a header over a coffee table.

At well after 11:00 p.m., back in our Country Coach, Teresa and I put an extra woolen blanket on the bed. January nights in Borrego Springs, we've learned, can be quite cold.

### Saturday, January 27

At 8:30 a.m. the next day, our campsites came alive. It was Chris's birthday, and we intended to celebrate in style. Chris and I set out in the Jeep, looking for cigars, but after four stops, the only stogies we found were at a dank, messy liquor store with mostly bare shelves. The last three cigars in Borrego Springs set us back a total of nine dollars.

Back at the campsite, Robert graciously offered to diagnose our hot water problem and quickly pinpointed the issue: operator error. Our Aqua-Hot hydronic heating system was bone dry of its necessary boiler antifreeze. Miraculously, I found a gallon of the stuff at a local hardware store. Robert soon restored our hot water system to operational equilibrium.

Meanwhile, at the adjoining campsite, preparations were underway for Chris's birthday lunch. Carla draped two outdoor picnic table with fresh tablecloths. Chris and Sandy teamed up on a Bloody Mary bar, Chris furnishing the vodka and tomato juice, Sandy setting out a mouthwatering array of garnishes: shrimp, bacon strips, pickle spears, horseradish, olives, cubes of cheese and bits of salami.

Carla served a beautiful egg frittata with potato, onion, kale, and roasted peppers. She had turned the previous night's leftover rib eye steaks into a tasty beef hash, and

*A product of the Bloody Mary bar*

Teresa's leftover vegetable tian again found its way to
the table. For dessert, Debbie served strawberries and
raspberries. After lunch, Chris, Robert, and I sat in the
warm sunshine and smoked those cheap cigars. We doused
the harsh aftertaste with lusty swigs of ice-cold beer from
tall cans of Miller High Life. John, a reformed cigarette
smoker, abstained from having a cigar, but his witty
conversation never flagged. He drank scotch.

We spent the rest of the day at the pool, reading and napping in the sun. From our horizontal position on the desert floor, the views of the looming San Ysidro Mountains were astonishing.

As dusk fell and the temperature dropped, Teresa and I showered and dressed for dinner. Thanks to Robert, our hot water troubles were behind us. Teresa and Carla worked together in the galley, creating a zesty Caesar salad, which we carried to Robert and Sandy's campsite. To our surprise, Robert and Sandy had elected to eat alfresco, despite the cold night. The outdoor lighting around their Prevost bus was stunning. A few extra jackets and Chris, Carla, Teresa, and I were good to go.

Robert grilled enormous Alaskan halibut fillets. He'd caught the fish himself and had it flash frozen and shipped to his home near San Diego. Robert is an accomplished chef. His garlic and onion sauce on the halibut, along with Teresa's Caesar, made for a memorable dinner. The wine flowed. Sandi put out two bowls of guacamole, which Chris and I reduced to rubble.

### Sunday, January 28

We awoke at 8:30 to another clear, windless morning. We took a long stroll through the RV park and then through an adjoining mobile home park. The compact lots were situated around a well-manicured executive golf course. The citrus on the mature trees—enormous grapefruits, lemons and oranges—made our eyes pop. We stopped in at the clean though somewhat dated clubhouse and were greeted by a friendly white-haired woman who was setting up for a memorial luncheon—one of their long-time, well-liked neighbors in the trailer park had recently passed. From the pictures on the posters, he looked like a fun guy—one of us, even.

Back at the RV park, standing alongside his gleaming Prevost bus, Robert was grilling thick burger patties. Teresa contributed roasted asparagus soup and a pack of Old Wisconsin polish sausages to the impromptu lunch. Carla passed around what remained of the previous day's frittata. Robert's burgers were huge. It was a good and filling meal. After lunch I lay on the bed in our Country Coach, and to the gentle hum of the air conditioning, I took a long nap.

*Burgers for lunch*

Later in the day, while Robert and John treated their wives to a round of margaritas at the swanky Casa Del Zorro resort, Chris and I set out in the Jeep for the liquor store (again). Chris was out of Tito's vodka, a near-fatal condition on a camping trip. We bought more wine. As the sun fell behind the rugged mountains, Teresa and I took a dip in the resort's swimming pool. While there, we couldn't help but bask a few minutes in one of the hot mineral baths. Robert and Sandy settled into the roiling spa next to ours. Robert was disgusted with himself for having put our six-pound prime rib roast on his new smoker too early in the day.

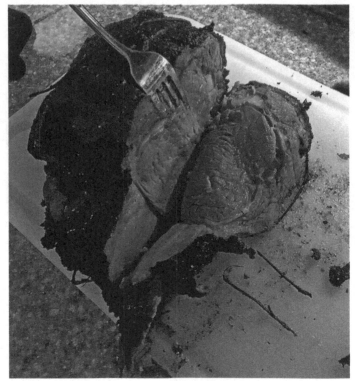

*Smoked to perfection*

*Warding off the evil spirits*

At 6:00 p.m., the cocktail flag went up. Teresa and I were hosting the prime rib dinner at our coach. Teresa put out beef-and-veal meatballs as a starter. Chris and Carla had recently spent a weekend at the Sparrows Lodge, a restored 1950s, 20-room retreat in Palm Springs. Chris lit incense from the Lodge and waved it around to ward off evil spirits. It apparently worked. Robert's prime rib roast was delicious and perfectly cooked, and to my knowledge, not a single evil spirit found its way into our coach. The end-of-night wine-bottle tally was par for this group: eight bottles.

**Monday, January 29**

Departure day. No walk this morning, no time even for breakfast. High winds were forecast for I-8, the Kumeyaay Highway, between Jacumba Hot Springs and Alpine, our route home. We wanted to get through the pass before the CHP closed the road to high-profile vehicles.

Robert and Sandy were first to leave. At our campsite, they alighted from their growling Prevost to say goodbye. John and Debbie left next. They swung their imposing coach east toward Arizona, planning to spend the rest of the week at the Phoenix Open golf tournament. Chris and Carla caravanned with us out of Borrego Springs, through the wasteland of Ocotillo Wells and the stop-and-go streets of El Centro, and finally west on I-8.

Our three-hour run home to San Diego was marked by strong winds at the higher elevations, but behind the wheel of our heavy Country Coach, the gusts felt like little more than a gentle tailwind. We reached Otay Mesa at 4:00 p.m. Teresa and I filled the back of our Jeep with food, dirty laundry, leftover booze, and hanging clothes, all to be sorted out at home. We left the coach in the capable hands of the crew at Big Toy Depot and joined the slog of evening commuters inching home as darkness fell.

Not glamorous, but it's how these trips generally end.

Vintage charm in the cozy library

## The Arizona Inn

If ever you wish to experience hotels in quantity, buy a motorhome.

They break down. Repairing one can take days or weeks, sometimes even months.

This means a lot of time in hotels.

But the news isn't all bad. Were it not for our 42' Country Coach Lexa and its quirky, failure-prone window latches and some seductive equipment upgrades, Teresa and I never would have made the acquaintance of the Arizona Inn, a sublime 92-room hotel in the heart of Tucson.

Thick walls, oak timbers, stone columns, lavishly furnished public rooms with enormous wood-burning fireplaces—this jewel of a property holds its own as one of the great overnight retreats in the American West.

The Arizona Inn opened for business on December 18, 1930. The hotel's early guests reached Tucson by train. Most of the Inn's rooms have oversized closets, designed to accommodate multiple steamer trunks and enough clothes to last the season.

Here's a sampling of the Inn's famous guests: Spencer Tracy and Katharine Hepburn, Clark Gable, Cary Grant, Frank Sinatra, John Wayne, Bob Hope. One junior senator

from Massachusetts, John F. Kennedy, reportedly enjoyed a
stay at the Inn and left his bathing suit behind. Raise your
hand if you think there's more to that story....

Another engaging storyline of the Inn is the biography
of its founder, Isabella Greenway. A self-described New Deal
Democrat, she served as Arizona's first congresswoman.
The twice-widowed, can-do entrepreneur and business-
woman born in Boone County, Kentucky, was a bridesmaid
in Eleanor Roosevelt's wedding. When Isabella built the Inn,
she insisted the floors be triple-layered to eliminate creaks.

On one dark, memorable night in Tucson, while our
Country Coach was beached in a cavernous service bay
at a local RV repair shop, Teresa and I checked in to the
Arizona Inn. The friendly desk staff winked as they gave
us our room key—an upgrade to a favored room called
The Treehouse for its second-story deck, which has a
sweeping view of the Catalina Mountains.

We quickly unpacked our things in the spacious,
welcoming guest room, oblivious to the dramatic view that
awaited us in daylight. We took a walk through the fragrant,
amply lit grounds and back to the main building, where
we peeked into the library, a plush, oak-timbered refuge
with hardwood floors and a blazing fire. The seating areas
were inviting: leather wingback chairs, overstuffed sofas,
rugs in a decidedly Southwestern motif. The books on the
floor-to-ceiling shelves were suitably dusty. The American
cherrywood cabinet in the corner, it was said, came from
Isabella Greenway's house in Santa Barbara.

Across the way, we found the Audubon Bar and Patio,
a perpetually busy watering hole that we suspect serves
as the informal outpost to the faculty lounge at nearby

*The furnished deck of The Treehouse boasts a sweeping view of the Catalina Mountains*

University of Arizona. The mature clientele was tastefully dressed: colorful scarves, skirts and layered sweaters for the ladies; coats, slacks and more than a few bow ties for the men. The rattan furniture was arranged around a tall potted palm in the center court.

Teresa and I timed our arrival exactly right. We snagged two coveted seats at the bar. Though a Manhattan is my go-to cocktail in most hotel bars, I instead bit on the Arizona

*The Main Dining Room*

Inn Old Fashioned, which is listed on the drink card
(Four Roses Bourbon, Angostura bitters, orange twist, and
a Luxardo maraschino cherry). It was superbly prepared by
our bartender, an affable young man named Sullivan, and I
had another, just to be certain Sullivan's first wasn't a fluke.

The Arizona Inn's Main Dining Room, a hushed, AAA
Four-Diamond restaurant, serves dinner until 9:30 p.m.—
it's one of the things we like about it. Another is its classic
menu: French onion soup, chilled vichyssoise, lobster
corn chowder, Caesar salad, duck breast, grilled lamb loin
chops, beef bourguignon, braised short ribs. For you native
Southern Californians, there's also seared salmon and
diver scallops.

We put the menu through its paces. My French onion
soup had a thick layer of gruyère cheese and was sweetened
with just the right amount of dry sherry. The Caesar had a

good kick. Our attentive server, Melody, was quick to bring
extra anchovies.

The oak-timber trusses overhead, a fire snapping and
popping in the corner fireplace, the white tablecloth with
its glittering flatware—the romantic atmosphere demanded
beef entrées accompanied by a bold, full-bodied cabernet
sauvignon. I was thrilled to discover one of our all-time
favorites on the wine list—a Frank Family Cabernet
(Napa Valley, 2014).

Teresa ordered the beef bourguignon—the meat
and vegetables came out properly tender, and the velvety
chorus was loaded with notes of cognac, bacon, and onion.
I couldn't resist trying the short ribs, which came highly
recommended. The ribs were well-marbled and full of
flavor, served over a creamy polenta, with enough rich wine
sauce left at the end to justify tearing chunks of ciabatta
bread and mopping up the muss. Stuffed to the gills and
borderline light-headed, I was at that desperate point of
pushing back from the table when Melody surprised us
with a plate of desserts. The medley included a piece of
dark chocolate cake, a *crème brûlée*, a mousse cup, and a
square of cheesecake.

"Shoot me now," I thought as we reduced the pastry
chef's selections to morsels.

We closed the dining room. Groaning, I followed
Teresa into the night, my shirt buttons strained to the point
of popping. With the feebleness of an extremely fat man,
I lumbered up the concrete stairs to our room.

The Treehouse had a king-sized sleigh bed. I stretched
out and slept soundly, dreaming of duck breast and baby
lamb chops.

We awoke to a brilliantly blue Arizona sky, a newspaper at our door. From our sundeck, the promised view of the Catalina Mountains was absorbing: steep rocky cliffs and deep, dark ravines, the sand-colored mountains jagged at the top. The sun was already hot.

I checked in with our RV repairman. The Country Coach was ready, but I bought us a little more time. We took a stroll through the fastidious grounds, past the citrus trees and vibrant flowers, the swimming pool and tennis courts, the wedding fountain and cactus gardens, the manicured lawns and pink cottages, until we found ourselves back at the Main Dining Room, being seated for breakfast.

The dining room was quiet. A fire burned in the fireplace. Over coffee, we perused the menu. My smoked salmon eggs Benedict arrived with the two poached eggs cooked to perfection. They were shaped like flying saucers, and their bright yellow yolks were runny at the touch of a fork. The salmon was lox-style, meaning cured but not smoked. It had a silky, oily texture and was satisfyingly salty. The hollandaise sauce, sown with plenty of lemon and vinegar, was buttery enough to beat any hangover. I licked my plate clean.

Over several more cups of coffee, I tried reading the newspaper but couldn't make heads or tails of it—all the bleating about things gone haywire in a world that suddenly seemed so far away.

On the Arizona Inn's opening night in 1930, Isabella Greenway promised her guests privacy, quiet, and sunshine. Ninety years later, her heirs are still fulfilling that promise.

It's amazing what you can experience traveling in a motorhome.

*Cessna Citation Sovereign ready to roll*

# Picnic at 41,000 Feet

Rich people fly first class. Stupendously rich people fly on private jets.

Being an independent author and publisher, I am neither rich nor smart, but I am occasionally lucky. Earlier this summer, luck afforded me the opportunity to fly out of Sitka, Alaska, on a private jet.

No check-in lines, no hectoring TSA agents, no shrieking children and germ-addled adults sneezing in confined spaces—flying private, I soon learned, is the only way to go.

Sitka is a city of 10,000 and is known primarily for three things: it's where the Alaska Purchase was signed, it was Alaska's first state capital, and it's only accessible by boat or air. Small as it is, Sitka's Rocky Gutierrez Airport has a separate terminal for its private aviation traffic. Most airports do. People who fly on private jets are generally unaccustomed to holding their own umbrella or driving their own car—why would they mingle with the unwashed masses?

Waiting for me in the private terminal was a fit man in a pilot's uniform. His name was John, and he had that serious military bearing. I found his solemn manner reassuring. You don't want to be hurtling through space at 495 miles an hour in a hell cart piloted by a nutjob who looks like

Guy Fieri. Captain John quickly relieved me of my roller bag and escorted me through two automatic glass doors to the tarmac, where a gleaming white jet stood waiting.

This flight was operated by NetJets, the largest private jet operator in the world and a pioneer in the business of fractional aircraft ownership. NetJets has some 750 aircraft under management. More than 7,000 uber-wealthy owners enjoy access to this fleet by paying colossal sums in advance. Trips can be scheduled at extremely short notice. Famed investor Warren Buffet was once one of these fractional owners, and he liked the service so well he bought the company.

Our jet was a Cessna Citation Sovereign. Four stairs extended from a clamshell-style door. Captain John stood aside as I mounted the steps and ducked into the cabin. The width of the jet's cabin was roughly that of a Cadillac Escalade. The height was a hair under six feet—once inside I had to crouch and shuffle to my seat.

*Luxurious double-club seating*

The cabin's interior, accented with glossy brown burl wood and bedecked in white leather and plush beige carpet, had that new-car smell. There were eight leather chairs arranged in two groupings of four, a layout NetJets calls double-club seating. The drink holders and ashtrays were brushed gold. We wore our seat belts fastened low over our hips and across a shoulder, like in a car.

From my seat facing forward, I had a direct view of the cockpit. There was no flight-deck door, like you'd see on a commercial airliner. In a matter of minutes we left the tarmac and taxied to the runway. I watched through the cockpit's windshield as though seated in a jump seat behind the pilot.

*View of the cockpit*

*Sitka is accessible only by boat or air*

Positioned for takeoff, the length of the runway stretching before us like a big empty freeway, our jet engines roared. John and his copilot stood on the brakes, restraining the quivering jet while they went through their final checklist. Finally, the nose dipped, and we hurtled down the runway. Next thing I knew, we rotated off the runway and began climbing at a steep angle. Looking behind me, the narrow strip of land that was the Sitka airport grew smaller and smaller.

At 10,000 feet, every NetJet has Wi-Fi service. There were ample universal power outlets throughout the cabin. Each seat grouping shared a generously sized burl wood desk that extended from the wall. The tranquil interior and the snowcapped mountain peaks out the window encouraged thoughtful work or deep meditation.

Our flight was less than two hours, barely time enough to catch lunch. I was curious. What do these modern-day jet-setters eat when they fly? Whatever my lunch, I intended to put it through its paces. This is, after all, a food column.

Unlike most of the high-end, vintage private railroad cars I've been privileged to travel on, our private jet had no galley, no chef, and no stewardess. Food was entirely self-service from a built-in refreshment center near the cockpit. Unwrapping my lunch, which came on a white plastic tray thoroughly covered in cellophane, was like unwrapping a mummy.

*Food was entirely self-service*

The lunch itself consisted of a small serving of potato salad and an equally small serving of fruit salad, a bag of chips, two quarters of a smoked ham and cheese sandwich, and a brownie wrapped in its own abundance of cellophane. The utensils that came packaged with the meal appeared to be made of real silver but proved to be lightweight plastic. I suspect Warren Buffet has invested in a cellophane and plastics company, too.

The makings for my self-service Bloody Mary were what I might expect at a tailgate party: get a clear plastic cup, scoop your own ice, grab a room-temperature can

*A Bloody Mary you'd expect at a tailgate party*

of Mr. & Mrs. T Original Bloody Mary Mix, and take an airline-size bottle of Grey Goose, which came in a unique, elongated design I hadn't seen before.

Once I returned to my seat and mixed my Bloody Mary, it was time to eat. The potato salad was creamy and mustardy. It came with nice chunks of potato. The fruit was hit-or-miss: strawberries a bit sour, cantaloupe sweet and satisfying with notes of honey, blueberries bone-dry and pasty, honeydew succulent and pleasingly moist. As you might guess, the turnkey Bloody Mary met the standards of a run-of-the-mill bowling alley, but it beat flying stone-cold sober.

Next, I tucked into the ham and cheese sandwich. The two sesame seed sandwich rolls were hard and surprisingly cool. (This jet had flown in from Aspen, Colorado, and Nashville before that. I suspect our box lunches were loaded onto the plane at one of these previous stops and stored in a refrigerated compartment.) The layered slices of ham were an inch thick, and the cheddar cheese slices were generous. I am a fan of spicy mustard, and fortunately my box lunch came with a 2-fluid-ounce bottle of Heinz Dijon mustard and a small bottle of Heinz mayonnaise.

Now if only there were similar-sized servings of horse-radish, Tabasco, and Lea & Perrins Worcestershire Sauce to spice up the Bloody Mary.

After eating my sandwich, still taking pulls of my Bloody Mary, I turned my attention to my bag of Metro Deli Sea Salt & Vinegar Potato Chips. The chips were gratifyingly salty and had a good snap. When I thought no one was watching, I licked the sea salt from my fingertips.

The brownie, which came without a label, turned out to be more like a small square of German chocolate cake.

It was topped with a grid-like pattern of chocolate frosting. As I ate my brownie it crumbled, and spongy chunks of chocolate fell exuberantly into my lap. I collected the chunks piece by piece, the dexterity of my fingers tested by a vodka haze.

*Snowcapped Alaska mountains*

Soon the wash of the jet engines and the heavy lunch were lulling me to sleep. I slept hard, only to be awakened by a sudden change in the engine noise. We were descending, already on approach to our destination runway.

Discretion is a hallmark of NetJet travel. The name of my host and our exact destination shall remain confidential, but for purposes of finishing this chronicle, I can tell you that upon landing, our jet taxied to three waiting rental cars, which were parked on the tarmac with their trunks open. Our bags were quickly transferred to the cars, and we left the tarmac in a mini-motorcade.

Passing through the security gate, I took one last look at the Citation in my rearview mirror, knowing I might never travel this way again. We entered a parking lot, which led to a frontage road, which took us to a busy thoroughfare and back to the real world.

Here's my takeaway: you may not be able to travel like a one-percenter, but for the price of a picnic lunch you can always eat like one.

*Turtle Bay Resort sits atop the northernmost point of Oahu*

# Blown Away in Oahu

When Charles Dickens penned the words, "It was the best of times, it was the worst of times," he must have been writing about a Christmas vacation spent with his family in Hawaii, because I felt pretty much the same way after taking my family to Oahu over the holidays.

The piped sounds of slack-key guitars, the rum-soaked cocktails in oversized glasses, the sugar-sand beaches adorned with lava rocks and tiki torches—the fantasy of a tropical paradise is catnip to the average American who's looking for a relaxing vacation. Is it any wonder they flock to Hawaii at Christmastime?

What these naïve vacationers fail to understand is that their pineapple drinks and overpriced hotel rooms are likely to come with nightmarish amenities: fistfights for beach chairs, first-degree sunburns, body welts from sand fleas, and daily muggings both figurative and literal.

Since we didn't want to waste our short vacation time traveling to an outer island, and since the best Waikiki hotels were full, I booked rooms at Turtle Bay Resort, on Oahu's North Shore. The boxy white hotel sits prominently on a point high above the ocean, enduring hurricane-force winds that seem to blow constantly, at least in late December.

The hotel was built in the early 1970s by casino developer Del Webb, who hoped to introduce the island's first casino, but the state's gaming initiative never passed. Today, the old hotel's wheel-and-spoke design and cavernous ground-floor lobby make it easier for roving bands of children to evade supervision by their parents.

We checked in to the hotel late in the afternoon on Christmas day. Hungry, thirsty, and irritable from our full day of travel, we made a beeline for one of Turtle Bay's on-site restaurants, Roy's Beach House. The small, overcrowded bar tested our patience. After waiting what seemed like an eternity, we finally got drink service and enough food to stave off a family mutiny, but we had to step on a lot of feet to make it happen. The servings were small and the prices were large. The Kahana-style tiger shrimp, Szechuan baby back pork ribs, and calamari went quickly, as did our first round of mai tais.

At 8:15 p.m. we were back at Roy's for Christmas dinner. Despite a long-standing apprehensiveness about this particular chain—I once nearly fainted after getting a glimpse into the back of a Roy's kitchen on an outer island—I found solace in the open-air, teakwood dining room of this attractive restaurant, which is mere steps from the breaking waves. The heavy-handed Polynesian decor might have been a Disneyland ride, but who cares? The rube reviewers of Yelp have given this Roy's four out of five stars, which is probably about what it deserves. I drank a lot of gin martinis and wine, and the pork ribs, shrimp cocktail, Caesar salad, and rack of lamb made for a happy, festive holiday dinner with the family.

*The obligatory holiday mai tai, garnished with an orchid
and served in a hurricane glass*

The next morning, we didn't need an alarm clock
to wake us up. The hammering wind and driving rain
that pelted our balcony slider were alarm enough. Teresa
and I met our daughters, Caroline and Katie, and Katie's
husband, Lucas, downstairs for coffee. The rain had trans-
formed the peaceful, would-be casino ground floor into
a school gymnasium on rainy day schedule: kids ran in
every direction, malicious teenagers loitered in packs,
young parents in tight-fitting athletic apparel cut through
the crowd pushing double strollers, their contrary infants
howling bloody murder. The line for Starbucks went forever.

Ah, Christmas in Hawaii.

*Howling winds and heavy surf bring flotsam and jetsam to the north-facing beaches*

Thinking weather conditions had to be better on the lee side of the island, I ordered everyone into our rented, government-black GMC Denali and asked Lucas to guide us to Waikiki Beach. Ramshackle describes much of the scenery through which we drove.

The gridlock we encountered on the south shore of the island was as bad as Southern California on any given day, but at least the view from our Denali improved dramatically as we neared Waikiki. My passengers stared wide-eyed at the idyllic panorama—the sunny skies and white sandy beaches, the high-rise beachfront hotels and their opulent, open-air lobbies, the chichi stores and ritzy restaurants.

My wife, daughters, and son-in-law instantly hated me for marooning them on Oahu's storm-swept North Shore.

I led our little band of travelers to the Halekulani, a five-star hotel, where we settled in for a long, leisurely lunch at the hotel's legendary restaurant, The House Without a Key. This indoor/outdoor fine-dining venue is named after Earl Derr Biggers's first Charlie Chan murder-mystery novel, which Biggers wrote in 1925 while staying at the Halekulani. The mai tais, coconut shrimp, tuna poke, fresh green salads, and multiple bottles of a dry white Italian wine nearly brought about my own murder—the exquisite setting and flavorful food underscored my incompetence as a travel planner. Who in his right mind books Turtle Bay at Christmas?

After lunch, like German tourists, we plodded single file through the sand in our street clothes, carrying our shoes.

In the wake of this ultimate humiliation, my family shunned me, again.

That night's dinner reservation did little to endear me to my doleful family. Weeks before, from my comfortable desk chair on the mainland, I had booked a table for five at Turtle Bay Resort's Kula Grill. In my haste to lock down dinner reservations, I failed to pick up on the coded phrase that is the death knell of any dinner establishment: kids eat free. Apparently, so do boorish foreigners.

As if the squalling children and obnoxious adults weren't bad enough, the lighting in this grill-cum-cafeteria was bright—bright enough to dig a splinter from the palm of your hand with a sewing needle, if you had to.

It was while seated at the Kula Grill, struggling to get through a half rack of mushy baby back pork ribs, that I had an out-of-body experience. The ghost of Christmas future, a Grim-Reaper-type figure dressed in a black hood and a long coat of rusty chains, led me to the dining room of another brightly lit restaurant. It was either a Red Lobster or an Olive Garden. The ghost pointed his bony finger at two seniors: Teresa and I were much older, and we were eating dinner at five o'clock. We had a coupon for a free dessert. I woke up screaming.

The next morning the sun came out, but I spoiled our kids' first decent beach day by agreeing to meet some dear family friends for lunch in the nearby town of Haleiwa. In the bumper-to-bumper traffic, the twelve-mile drive took us more than an hour.

Once we finally got there, the small storefront restaurant Opal Thai was a highlight of our time on Oahu. We sat inside on a wooden picnic table. Opal, the owner, was more ringmaster and game-show host than restaurateur. Charismatic and funny, he entertained his patrons as he polled them for their gustatory preferences, and then without taking orders, he brought trays of food from the kitchen. The dishes Opal brought to our table were mostly shrimp and seafood. The flavors—sweet, sour, spicy, salty—left us dazzled. The green beans were remarkable.

We all groaned when Opal delivered a second wave of food, including a "chef's special" that turned out to be skate. We left happy and stuffed. Opal saw us out with handshakes, fist bumps, and hugs for each of the ladies.

By 4:00 p.m. Katie, Lucas, and Caroline were back on the beach. Teresa and I soon joined them, wallowing on two chaises in the white sand under an umbrella. When the long shadow of the hotel fell across the beach, we retreated to our rooms for showers. We stuck with our one sure thing:

another dinner at Roy's. My New Zealand king salmon was good, but what made the night memorable were the chuckleheads we met in the bar: two middle-aged brothers dead-drunk and doing Jagerbombs. One from Colorado, one from Wisconsin, they could barely stand. Their father, they said, was a Stanford football coach.

The next day, the good weather held, and we passed the time under a beach umbrella, drinking piña coladas and mai tais. We took turns ordering lunches at the takeout window at Roy's. The kitchen was perpetually backed up. It took me more than thirty minutes to collect an order of chicken wings, a cheeseburger, and fries. Teresa and I split the chicken wings and the cheeseburger. I gave the fries to a three-year-old boy who was hungry to the point of tears— his mother was still waiting for the food she'd ordered some forty-five minutes earlier.

*When good weather held, we were back on the beach*

By this time we'd discovered Lei Lei's, Turtle Bay's golf
course grill. When we looked in on this casual restaurant,
Ian, the outgoing, amiable owner—a former Chart House
guy—shamed us into canceling our reservation at Turtle
Bay's celebrated Pa'akai seafood restaurant and eating at
Lei Lei's instead.

Lucky us. Ian's menu, reminiscent of Chart House fare,
was wonderful. We indulged our voracious appetites with
seared ahi sashimi, escargot, calamari, Caesar salads and
double-cut New York strip steaks. Lucas went for a 28 oz.
bone-in cut of Lei Lei's signature prime rib, which came out
with a juicy red center and a sturdy salt and pepper crust.
Katie, Lucas, and Caroline surprised Teresa and me with
a bottle of Chappellet Cabernet. It was a late celebration of
our wedding anniversary.

I felt unshunned, at last.

That night, while dining alfresco, we watched a band
of Lord-of-the-Flies nomad kids lay siege to the golf course's
putting green. They threw sprays of golf balls into the night,
they hammered sand rakes teeth-first into the fine grass,
they dug deep divots around the cups with the heels of
their bare feet. A recovering golfer and former golf camp
counselor, I sipped my martini and bit my tongue. I didn't
want to start an international incident. Their three sets of
parents spoke a language that sounded Middle Eastern.
In that part of the world, apparently, parents have no truck
with golf course etiquette.

Predictably, we returned to Lei Lei's the following
night. Thinking it might be fun to smoke a cigar on our
last night in Hawaii, Lucas and I had detoured into the golf
shop earlier in the day. Only a reckless squanderer would

pay what I paid for two Macanudos, but then how often do you get to smoke a cigar in Hawaii? On this quiet night, there were no unsupervised child mercenaries assaulting the property, and Lucas and I—son-in-law and father of the bride, respectively—enjoyed a quiet stroll around the darkened putting green as we puffed our expensive cigars. We talked golf, mostly.

The next day, at the Honolulu International Airport, our trip ended with a sharp slap in the face. The tab for our rented Denali, which we had all of five days, was $2,000. Inside the terminal, we ate cold sandwiches from a food cart. The boarding gate was mobbed with people. There were no seats to be had. Half of us fought flu symptoms.

There are only thirteen letters in the Hawaiian alphabet, and this apparently limits the number of words in their vocabulary. For example, *aloha* means both *hello* and *goodbye*—kind of like on a small-town high school football team, where some of the players go both ways. We finally boarded the crowded airliner.

"Aloha," I said, finding my seat, facing the ignominy of flying five hours in coach. I meant it as *goodbye*. As in, "It'll be some time before I return to Hawaii, and never again at Christmas."

Cue Dickens: It was the best of times, it was the worst of times. I take that back. Cue Poe: Nevermore North Shore.

A white-hulled 100-foot superyacht docked
at Gilford Island, British Columbia

# Overeating on a Superyacht

She was fit for a spread in a yachting magazine: a gleaming
white-hulled 100-foot superyacht, powered by twin Detroit
Diesels, her sleek profile tasteful yet somewhat sinister—a
floating stronghold from which James Bond's archenemy
might launch a takeover of the world.

It was late May, and the boat was making a nine-day
repositioning cruise from Gig Harbor, Washington, to
Ketchikan, Alaska, where her owners would spend the
summer cruising Alaska's Inside Passageway. By some
miracle, for this leg of the trip, one of her two guest
staterooms was offered to my brother, Chris, and the other
to me.

No internet, no television, no cell service, a private chef, a
chance to read books and write my novel undisturbed—it's a
wonder I didn't get a speeding ticket on the way to the airport.

### Tuesday, May 29

The day before boarding the boat, Chris and I met up at
Seattle's Edgewater Hotel, a long-in-the-tooth waterfront
property whose claim to fame is that the Beatles once stayed
there and fished from the open window of their hotel suite.
Chris and I neither sing nor fish, so we spent the afternoon

walking the hills of downtown Seattle. In late May, it still felt like winter.

Is any tourist trap photographed more than Pike Place Market?

For dinner, to get in the spirit, we saddled up to the long, colorful bar of a modern waterfront restaurant. At this time of year, being so far north, the days are long—eating dinner in broad daylight took some getting used to. The gin helped. My seafood stew was tasty but wanting in volume. The bartender, a would-be writer, learned that I had written a novel and promised to order a copy of my latest book. We bumped his tip—by about 4x my royalty on the book, I realized the next day.

### Wednesday, May 30

The next morning, leaving the Edgewater Hotel, Chris and I found ourselves in the shadow of a monstrosity. In the night, Norwegian Cruise Line's (NCL) newest megaship, *Norwegian Bliss*, had tied up next door. This behemoth blocked the sun; it was like staring up at the MGM Grand.

"It's their invitation-only, inaugural cruise," a middle-aged Canadian woman told us. "Mostly travel agents. Three days to Victoria and back. For free." She gave us her card. She was a travel agent.

I thought, "Except for book publishers, only cruise ship operators are lame-brained enough to give away their product for free to an audience that will trash it in snarky reviews."

The *Bliss* holds 4,000 passengers. On the top deck, along with the obligatory water park for the kiddies, is a 1,000-foot go-kart track.

Someone in Norway should be horsewhipped.

Over salmon tacos and clam chowder at a seafood restaurant called Anthony's, we watched the leeches and sponges of the travel-agency world board the grandiose ship. Most of the ship's passengers wheeled two roller bags—the second one, we surmised, for the ship's silver.

**Thursday, May 31**

Our superyacht departed Gig Harbor early the next day. Mark, the captain, adroitly operated the boat from the flying bridge while Sean, the mate, and John, the chef, handled the lines. The Peterson brothers were monkeys, pretending to help with the lines and getting wet.

Cruising north, we left Seattle behind us, crossed the Strait of Juan de Fuca, and checked in with Canadian customs at Bedwell Harbor. The attractive, vintage hotel overlooking the marina was Poet's Cove. The sun felt good on our faces. We anchored that night at Montague Bay, an hour north of Bedwell Harbor.

Aboard the boat, cocktail hour commenced every evening at 5:30. We gathered in the comfortable salon. That first night, for an appetizer, Chef John served a delectable chicken satay with peanut sauce. This was my idea of roughing it through the Great White North.

At 7:00 p.m. we moved to the formal dining table. Chef John's perfectly grilled filets of tenderloin beef and a fresh green salad were passed family style around the table.

After dinner, it was warm enough—and still light enough—to take a bottle of wine to the top deck. We drank from red solo cups. Coming back down the steep steps, I sloshed red wine on the white Berber carpet of the wheelhouse and spent the rest of the night on hands

*The chef at work on egg burritos*

and knees, scrubbing the stain with club soda and a kitchen towel.

### Friday, June 1

Early the next day, as we pulled anchor, the smell of bacon wafted from the galley.

"Stir sticks," we said, planting the strips of bacon in our red solo cups brimming with Bloody Marys. Captain Mark corrected us. In Canada, Bloody Marys are called *Caesars*. They're customarily made with Clamato, a reconstituted tomato juice flavored with spices and clam broth. In honor of Canada, I had two Caesars. The purr of the Detroit Diesels led to a late-morning nap.

On this trip, between meals—and naps—I sat at the dining table and worked on a new novel, a sequel to *The Dining Car*. The rain was constant. With so few distractions, my production as a writer eclipsed what I could do at home.

By this time, I was living in jeans and a heavy sweatshirt, and I was always barefoot when aboard the boat.

Late that day, docked at a marina at Campbell River, we found a grocery store within easy walking distance. Chris and I followed Chef John through the brightly lit aisles. Have you ever seen a real chef shop? It was as if John were running a steeplechase, families and shopping carts the obstacles.

Dinner that night was memorable: fried oysters, grilled halibut, potatoes, and a tossed green salad.

### Saturday, June 2

We left Campbell River on a rainy, windy morning. The low clouds, dense forests, and cascading waterfalls of the Seymour Narrows made for riveting scenery. During this scenic stretch, the pace of my writing slowed considerably.

Chef John served a delicious broccoli-and-beef filet Chinese stir-fry lunch.

*A delicious broccoli-and-beef filet Chinese stir-fry lunch*

That evening, docked at Echo Bay, Gilford Island, Mark introduced us to local Nikki van Schyndel, a world-recognized survivalist who made a name for herself by living (voluntarily!) nineteen months in the harsh elements of the British Columbia wilderness. (For a harrowing adventure tale, read Nikki's book *Becoming Wild*.)

It doesn't hurt that with her jet-black hair and sapphire blue eyes, Nikki looks like a young Elizabeth Taylor.

Nikki joined us at the boat's dining table, telling us the latest. Ironically, she's been drummed out of her burgeoning ecotourism business by the Canadian government for lacking the proper permits. If she's caught picking her trademark "wild" salads on Canada's nature preserves, the officials warned, she faces a $10,000 fine.

### Sunday, June 3

We left Echo Bay on a wet, gray morning. Entering the broad, deep waters of Queen Charlotte Strait, we caught sight of the cruise ships *Golden Princess* and *Nieuw Amsterdam*, both steaming north toward Ketchikan.

For our Sunday breakfast, Chef John had a decadent treat in store: chilaquiles, the traditional Mexican dish, made wickedly with salsa and mashed up Doritos. John served the scrambled eggs on the side.

A few hours later, our reward for successfully crossing the open waters of Queen Charlotte Sound, where for a time we bobbed like a cork on a roiling ocean, was a lavish taco salad.

I followed this fiesta of a lunch with a long nap in my darkened stateroom, which was appointed like a room at the Four Seasons Hotel.

*My opulent stateroom invited long naps*

Later that day, passing the Indian Reserve community of Bella Bella, we had a brief window of cell service. There was a scramble to catch up on email and call home before losing our signal again.

Mark took us up a majestic, narrow passage, where we anchored in an isolated bay while being pelted by torrential rains. During cocktail hour, when shafts of sunlight started breaking through the clouds, the rainbows were vivid.

*Bulgogi, a classic Korean barbecue dish*

That night, Chef John made beef bulgogi, a classic Korean barbecue dish. He served the impressive meal with wok-fried vegetables.

### Monday, June 4

Fueled by coffee, sausage, and eggs, I had a good morning of writing. The rain never let up. At noon, I broke away to feast on a pulled-pork sandwich.

In the afternoon, as we cruised through calm waters, I spent some time sitting with Captain Mark up in the wheelhouse. On our port side, a humpback whale breached.

Late in the day Mark found a quiet cove. We dropped
anchor and had a Thanksgiving-style turkey dinner, com-
plete with creamy mashed potatoes and gravy.

### Tuesday, June 5

The next morning, still at anchor and with a light rain
falling, Chef John served congee for breakfast. At first
I mistook this savory, rice-based dish for oatmeal, but the
subtle flavors of scallions and ginger quickly distinguished
this Asian standard from its Western counterpart.

I was by now in the routine of going to bed at 9:00 p.m.
and waking up at 6:00 a.m. I never saw the dark of night.

### Wednesday, June 6

Heavy winds, big rains in the night—the boat pitched and
rolled and pulled at its anchor. The morning was dark and
blustery. Our destination was Newcomb Harbor. We arrived
in more rain and gusting winds. Twelve-foot swells were
reported on Queen Charlotte Sound.

For me, it was another productive day of writing.
Chef John prepared a sumptuous dinner: rack of lamb
with potatoes and a Greek salad.

### Thursday, June 7

Awake and writing at 5:00 a.m. Breakfast in the galley:
blueberry pancakes, bacon, and eggs.

Clam chowder and garlic toast for lunch. Chris and
I had Bloody Marys. It was an easy sale. We kept telling
ourselves, "How often..." My ensuing nap was sublime.

Later that day, at anchor in a peaceful, rainy cove, we
watched a local fisherman work the waters around our boat.

He landed a halibut. The next thing I knew, he was backing his boat to our aft-deck and handing the big fish over to Captain Mark. Howard, our generous Canadian fisherman friend, gave us a bucket of prawns, too.

Chris saw what was happening and hailed Howard back, hoping to give him a bottle of wine as thanks.

"What do you like?" Chris called from the aft-deck. "Red or white?"

"White!" Howard shouted through cupped hands. "Anything but chardonnay!"

*Howard, the generous Canadian fisherman, trades seafood for wine. "No chardonnay!"*

**Friday, June 8**

Closing in on the port city of Prince Rupert, we had a sudden burst of cell service. It meant civilization was near. Our trip was ending.

At 2:00 p.m. we reached Ketchikan. The NCL cruise ship *Pearl*, southbound, was just leaving the harbor. The passage out was so narrow that we had to wait for the *Pearl* to pass before entering the channel. It made us wonder how a ship the size of *Norwegian Bliss* will ever negotiate these tight waters.

Our last dinner aboard the boat was a surf and turf served family style: Howard's prawns and halibut, carne asada with Búfalo-brand red sauce and salsa, steamed vegetables, a colorful green salad. The wine flowed.

**Saturday, June 9**

On this drizzly morning in Ketchikan, our last full day on the boat, Chris and I sat in the galley, drinking Bloody Marys and watching Chef John craft eggs Benedict. It was like watching a cooking show.

This was the afternoon our boat's owners flew in. As a thank-you to them and to the crew, Chris and I proposed taking everyone to dinner at Ketchikan's finest restaurant, the Cape Fox Inn. The restaurant is perched high on a mountainside and offers sweeping views of the harbor. Everyone assented. We were seated promptly for our reservation—it was 7:00 p.m.—at a big round table near a floor-to-ceiling picture window. We watched the cruise ships leave. First out was the Disney ship *Wonder*— Mickey Mouse ears on the red smokestacks and cartoons playing on a massive screen on the top deck.

With its list of predictable fare presented on menu pages laminated in plastic, with its laugh-out-loud wine list—third-rate labels I wouldn't even use for cooking—and with its questionable cuisine—my horseradish-encrusted salmon was so bland and bizarre, and so offensive to Chef John that he had words with the manager about it—the Cape Fox Inn was no fine-dining experience, but then again, we reminded ourselves, this was Ketchikan, not Paris.

### Sunday, June 10

On Sunday morning I awoke at 6:00, left my stateroom, and came up top. It was drizzling. Ahead of us, five gigantic cruise ships were docked.

For Chris and me, this was the end of the line. We packed our bags, stripped our beds, chugged a cup of coffee, wolfed down a satisfying egg burrito—Chef John had just pulled the pan from the oven—and said goodbye to our friends on the boat.

We reached Ketchikan's airport, on Gravina Island, by ferry. The scuttled Gravina Island Bridge project is infamously known as the "bridge to nowhere." The $398 million project, a poster child for pork barrel spending, never got built.

The airport is as tiny as the town it serves, but its TSA agents are Herculean. They wasted no time snatching Chris's briefcase from the conveyor belt.

"Mind if we take a look?" the woman demanded.

Upon returning the bag to Chris, who was halfway through an 850-page biography of J.P. Morgan and had the book stowed in his briefcase, the TSA agent offered an explanation.

"It seemed suspicious," she said. "Books that big don't normally come through Ketchikan."

*The islands abound with freshwater alpine lakes*

# Eating Out

*Union Station has been revitalized to include a luxury hotel*

# Denver Union Station

I couldn't imagine a more exciting phone call to get. My great friend Patrick Henry, owner of the private railroad cars *Warren R. Henry* and *Evelyn Henry,* had an offer too good to refuse. His luxurious train cars were scheduled to deadhead from Denver to Emeryville, California, on an upcoming California Zephyr, chef and onboard service manager included. Three couples could travel if I'd be willing to cover his expenses....

Of course, Teresa and I jumped at the opportunity, and we quickly recruited our accomplices from the "Private Varnish: A Birthday to Remember" trip that you may have read about earlier in this aimless series of essays.

We flew to Denver, where we met up with Pat, Susan, Chris, and the latest conscript to our wayward band of travelers, Chris's wife, Carla. We'd heard about the revitalization of Denver Union Station, and arriving a day early seemed the ideal opportunity to check it out.

A number of train stations on the Amtrak route have their claim to fame: Washington DC's Union Station has its beaux arts panache, Chicago Union Station its legendary Great Hall, Kansas City Union Station its dizzying events calendar and signature Freight House restaurants. In the west, Los Angeles Union Station has its Art Deco and Mission Revival architecture, and Portland, Oregon, its terra-cotta Romanesque architecture and 150-foot Seth Thomas clock tower that looms high above the city's Old Town Chinatown section.

But for success in every measure—architectural acclaim, commercial viability, cultural triumph—Denver Union Station stands alone. It is the only big-city train station in which I will gladly spend the night.

Credit a redevelopment effort that began in 2001.

A landmark public/private partnership coalesced behind an inspired master plan. I'll spare the reader the entire list of acronyms for the partner agencies that were involved (CCD, CDOT, DRCOG, FTA, USNC, DUSPA, to name a few), but the mixed-use plan, still taking shape, includes office, hotel, residential, and retail space.

The development boasts a long list of environmental features: a minimized footprint, the use of natural light and renewable energy sources, LEED certification, low-flow toilets (in a train station!), a pedestrian-friendly, multi-modal transit hub, including an underground bus station, and an innovative storm water management system.

Union Station Terminal opened for business in July 2014. Future phases include adding more office space, more hotel rooms, and expanding the reach of the light rail system, which now connects to Denver International Airport.

If I were young, I'd be sorely tempted to move to Denver. One garrulous and friendly transit supervisor told me they can't hire enough train operators to fill all the vacant positions.

From the airport, Teresa and I took a taxi to the historic Lower Downtown district, known as LoDo, and checked

in to the five-star Crawford Hotel, which is located on
the upper floors of Denver Union Station and sits regally
above several enticing bars, restaurants, and retail shops.
Its neighbors include Coors Field, the home of the Colorado
Rockies, the mile-long 16th Street Mall, a Whole Foods
Market, and the historic Oxford Hotel. The buildings in
this downtown district are mostly red brick. The streets
are impressively clean.

Our fourth-floor
suite, in what was
formerly the train
station's attic, still had
the original red brick
walls. The vaulted
ceilings, crystal
chandeliers, and
massive rough-hewn
beams brought to mind
the rustic, historic riches
of the Rocky Mountain
gold rush. The suite
featured high ceilings,
a separate seating area,
and the sort of airy,
glass-and-marble bath
that you'd expect to find
in a Four Seasons Hotel.

At the Crawford Hotel, rough-hewn
beams, crystal chandeliers, and
exposed brick give the guest rooms
a rustic sophistication

For its registered guests, the Crawford Hotel offers
pick up and drop off service anywhere around LoDo
in their courtesy car, a Tesla, but Teresa and I opted to
explore the neighborhood on foot. We began with a walk

around Union Station. We noticed first off that security
was reassuringly tight. Knots of Homeland Security agents,
all dressed in black and heavily armed, stood vigil at the
train station doors. Transit security officers, also armed,
scurried to meet arriving trains. Amtrak police were there
in force, too. Panhandlers were few and far between.

The seating in the main terminal is sophisticated, warm,
elegant, and plentiful. Soaring arched windows infuse
the space with natural light. The walls are painted white.
The chandeliers are golden. The terrazzo floor is pristine.
The air is filled with the fresh scents of roses, coffee, and
baking croissants—no trace of that musty old post-office
smell that permeates most train stations. Electrical outlets
are conveniently located in all the seating areas.

To my surprise, inside the terminal, we came across
a small but well-stocked bookstore. The Tattered Cover
Bookstore is the satellite operation of a much larger
bookstore bearing the same name, located nearby on 16th
Street. This Tattered Cover even had a "Trains" section
among its bookshelves. The only black mark: they didn't
stock my book, *The Dining Car*, but the delightful, Pulitzer
Prize winning novel I picked up there, *Less*, by Andrew
Sean Greer, was so funny and so well written that I forgave
them their lapse.

For this time in Denver, Chris served as our tour guide
and travel concierge. He led us to a late lunch at Hearth &
Dram, a self-described "whiskey-centric" modern saloon
and brick-rustic American restaurant a few blocks from
Union Station.

"A dram," Chris explained, "usually refers to a taste
of whiskey. It's more than a splash, less than a jigger."

*Inside Union Station's soaring Great Hall*

The bartenders at Hearth & Dram use a rolling librarian's ladder to retrieve more than 300 whiskeys on display from around the world.

Listed on the craft cocktail menu is one $350 cocktail. Its base ingredient is a healthy shot of Yamazaki 18-year-old Japanese single malt whiskey, considered by experts to be one of the top scotches in the world, but the good ol' boy in me shrugged it off. I was too busy staring at a line of labels high on the wall behind the bar but within easy reach of the bartender's ladder: several bottles of Sazarac Company's flagship brand of nearly-impossible-to-find bourbon, Pappy Van Winkle.

We passed on the pricey bourbon and spent our money on lunch: Cobb salads, a smoked pastrami Reuben, iced tea, fries. Chris insisted we add the award-winning H&D Burger to our order. What makes the burger special is its husky smack of umami—think the flavor of veal stock—that is neither sweet nor sour, neither salty nor bitter. We suspect the Hearth & Dram's chefs achieve this pinnacle realization of taste—some call it "yummy"—using sautéed mushrooms. The H&D Burger comes with thick-cut bacon and smoky cheddar cheese. To underscore the sandwich's mettle, our pleasant female server planted a heavy silver trophy at the center of our table, proof that this burger recently finished first in the highly competitive Denver Burger Battle.

As evening fell, Teresa and I were back in our comfortable room in the Crawford, dressing for dinner. We made it downstairs in time to watch Amtrak's eastbound California Zephyr depart for Chicago. It wasn't our train, but is there anything more exciting than watching a glistening silver double-decked passenger train leave a station? The tracks of Union Station are partially covered by enormous white canopies that float sail-like above the train platform, and at night the space is well-lit. It's the setting for a celebration of renewal: clean, modern, and happy.

Having successfully seen the Zephyr off, our party moved inside Union Station to the Cooper Lounge, which is situated like a well-kept secret above the din of the rabble, on the train station's mezzanine level. The Cooper Lounge

*Aesthetically pleasing canopies shield waiting train passengers
from the elements*

is a spectacularly glamorous bar with bright light, tasteful
furnishings, and a chichi clientele. Drinks are presented
on silver trays. We eschewed the fussy craft cocktails of
the menu for classic Tanqueray gin martinis—extra dry,
of course. The steak tartare and lollipops of Colorado lamb
were astonishing.

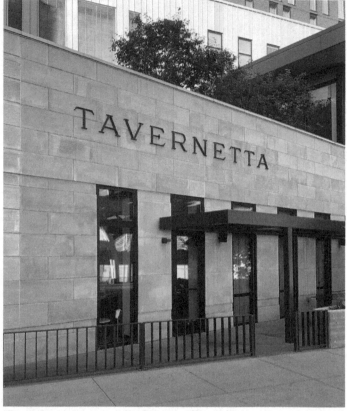

*The Italian restaurant Tavernetta offers la dolce vita style dining*

We then stumbled our way into Stoic & Genuine, one of Union Station's ground-floor restaurants featuring an open kitchen and a raw oyster bar. The bartender was attentive. The champagne flowed. Stoic & Genuine is an upscale seafood restaurant. We had a dozen oysters—a sampling of East and West Coast oysters—before signing the check and moving on to dinner at the swank, nearby Italian restaurant Tavernetta, which strives to deliver la dolce vita style dining to the energetic Union Station neighborhood.

Grass-fed beef carpaccio, lamb gnocchi, and Maine lobster; roasted quail, grilled lamb, and rare-cooked slices of a New York strip, summer vegetables and one too many Manhattans—and too much red wine—our extended dinner lasted into the night. If memory serves me correctly, we closed the restaurant.

The next morning at 8:00, the westbound Zephyr was backing down Track 5, about to couple to our two private railroad cars.

Standing on the station platform on this warm morning, one manicured hand on the handle of her roller bag, the other clutching a Starbucks, Teresa looked wistfully around at the white canopies casting their cool shade over the tracks, at the dormers of our sumptuous attic room in the Crawford Hotel, at the small, elegant patio of Tavernetta, which faces the tracks.

"Do we have to go?" she asked.

My preferred dinner destination is a top-tier chophouse

# Fine Dining in the iPhone Generation

It's an insidious practice—upscale restaurants are increasingly serving small plates in lieu of properly portioned entrées. If the trend continues, a generation of diners will be permanently saddled with the palates of dilettantes and the appetites of Lilliputians. Fine dining in the traditional sense will go the way of the Princess rotary-dial phone.

I confess to being a dinosaur. When setting out for a night on the town, my destination is invariably a top-tier chophouse: dim lighting, white linen tablecloths, a full bar, and food portions that guarantee I'll walk out groaning.

This being my reference, you can imagine my horror when an online restaurant-industry trade magazine crossed my desk, and the feature article extolled the virtues of small, shareable seafood plates. According to the newsletter, called *Restaurant Hospitality Eat Beat*, the craze for small bites was hitting trendy, upscale restaurants in a big way.

"Small plates are really good because we're in an iPhone world and our attention spans are getting smaller and smaller as time goes on," said restaurateur and *Top Chef* finalist Brian Malarkey, whose small plate of Buffalo octopus "stole the show" at the Sundance Film

Festival this year, according to the newsletter. "The days of giant steaks and big fish are done," Malarkey added. "It's now one bite of this, one bite of that. I can't get three bites into something before I'm like, 'What's next?'"

At this point, reading at my desk, I grew faint. The next thing I knew, my assistant was waving smelling salts under my nose and helping me off the floor.

The trend toward small-plate, prix fixe menus is incontrovertible. Such celebrated establishments as Benu, Chez Panisse, and The French Laundry all follow the despotic formula of "you'll get what the chef gives you, and that's that." But then, so does the state prison at San Quentin.

What galls me is that these chef-driven restaurants are so unapologetic about their approach to fine dining. Its an affront to American tradition, a healthy appetite, and personal choice. On its website, The French Laundry says, "We serve a series of small courses meant to excite your mind, satisfy your appetite and pique your curiosity. We want you to say, 'I wish I had just one more bite of that.' And then the next plate arrives and the same thing happens."

I have to ask myself, has the restaurant world gone stark raving mad?

I was beginning to think yes—that is, until one weekend, when my travels took me to Santa Cruz, California, for a wine-bottling weekend high in the mountains. On Sunday we had a late-afternoon plane to catch, and this gave my traveling companions and me the opportunity to grab an early lunch near the airport.

The restaurant we quite inadvertently stumbled upon in downtown San Jose was Original Joe's Italian Restaurant,

*At Original Joe's, you'll find 117 items on the menu*

a descendant of the Original Joe's founded in San Francisco
in 1937.

Low lighting, crescent leather booths, white linen tablecloths under a cavernous ceiling—this was a *real* restaurant.
Our server, Jose Luis, wore a tuxedo. He was perhaps sixty
years old. In his twenty-nine years at Original Joe's, he had
personally tasted every one of the menu's 117 items. He
wasn't so fond of the sweetbreads or the liver, he said, but
the spaghetti, lasagna, and minestrone soup were excellent.

"The prime rib is ready to be served," Jose Luis added.
It was 11:30 in the morning.

At Original Joe's, the omelets are made with four
eggs. Order bacon and eggs, and you get crispy stout steak
fries and a truckload of bacon with your scrambled eggs.
The Bloody Marys arrive nearly colorless at the top. And the
sheer girth of the club sandwiches being portaged through

the dining room made our eyes pop. Imagine what dinner must be like.

Here's my advice to those of you in the iPhone generation who are putting down a credit card and waiting two to three months for a table at some small-plate, prix fixe nirvana of gustatory endeavor. Cancel your reservation. Use what you save to spring for an Uber. Go to Original Joe's in San Jose, where a gentlemanly server in a tuxedo will unobtrusively attend to your every need. You'll eat what you want, and you won't go away hungry.

Chew on that with your minuscule plate of Buffalo octopus, chef Brian Malarkey.

*Unless you're the dining room of the Waldorf Astoria...*

## The Menace of Music

The human animal is growing increasingly barbaric by the day, and I've got the evidence to prove it—loud music in upscale restaurants.

Unless you're the dining room of the Waldorf Astoria New York, and unless you have a string quartet playing Haydn, I don't want to hear it—not your overamplified jazz or your folksy guitarist imitating the Eagles, or, god forbid, your damn karaoke machine with the amateurs at the microphone, shrieking like cats.

What commonsensical person would patronize such a place?

I've stopped frequenting one favorite watering hole because they offer live jazz seven nights a week. My wife and I loved this place when it first arrived on the scene. It was an easy walk from our high-rise condominium in San Diego's Marina District. The restaurant's luxuriously appointed, glittering décor made it one of the most welcoming dining destinations in town, the staff was friendly and accommodating, and the bar was blissfully quiet.

Now I can't stand the place. Live jazz *seven nights a week*! The electronic caterwauling is inescapable, even when one flees to the upstairs dining room. I won't name the place—it starts with Eddie and ends with V—but it has me scratching my head. Does management really not understand what a menace this preposterously deafening music represents, and how it drives people away?

*It starts with Eddie and ends with V*

Ah, Peterson, you wishful thinker.

We all know instinctively that loud music in an upscale restaurant conveniently shields legions of well-heeled halfwits from engaging in meaningful social interaction the way gin and tonics once shielded British officers from malaria. The sad fact is, the level of socio-functional illiteracy in our society is alarmingly high. People simply don't know how to talk to one another.

For far too many, a night on the town is a summons for an assault on the senses. We've all been there. The music blasts. Drink orders are shouted at the nearest bartender, who can't hear. Patrons are reduced to pointing stupidly to some inane craft cocktail listed on the gimmicky bar menu.

Meanwhile, the guests at the tables have their noses planted firmly in their iPhones, checking their latest Facebook feed and tabulating *likes* and *follows* on their Instagram app. Don't even get me started on Tik Tok.

For legions of dolts giving wide berth to all things serious and noble—like good conversation in a quiet chophouse, where you can still get a properly portioned meal   food in one of these raucous rathskellers is likely to be an afterthought. Dinner might consist of three share plates of fried goat-cheese balls, baked shishito peppers, and a beet-carrot éclair, after which everyone files home to turn on their 60″ flat-screen TV and catch the latest episode of *The Real Housewives of New Jersey.*

To this day, my inclination toward seasickness as a boy makes me reluctant as a grown man to board a boat unless it's the *Queen Mary 2* making a transatlantic crossing, which is preferable to flying. Similarly, my revulsion for loud music makes it impossible for me to attend a rock concert.

Had Teresa, a lifelong lover of music, known what a stodgy curmudgeon I'd become with respect to rock and roll, she'd have married Glen Frey instead.

Call me hypersensitive but sitting in a bleacher seat for three hours is disconcerting enough. Having people standing all around me, singing lyrics at the top of their lungs, leaves me with the urge to stick my head in an oven and turn up the gas.

I put this out there, gratis, to the music industry. Here's the perfect rock concert: Your famous band plays one song, preferably their most popular hit. Then they take a sixty-minute break, during which time a battalion of servers circulates through the crowd, bearing trays of cut crystal flutes brimming with Veuve Clicquot, weighty tumblers of Johnnie Walker Blue, and foie gras canapés. In this quiet interlude, the audience engages in conversation about art, literature, architecture, the best hotels of the world, and the most desirous destination parks for class "A" motorhomes.

The band returns for one last song—their second biggest hit, a tune with which we're all somewhat familiar. The audience neither stands nor sings. After this, the band leaves the stage, and there is no curtain call. The battalion of servers returns, though, offering more champagne and scotch. Cigars have supplanted the trays of foie gras. Throughout the venue, restrooms are pristine and easily accessed.

The cost for a ticket to this concert would be $3.98—about what you'd pay to purchase the same two songs on iTunes.

Make it Conway Twitty, if you would, or John Denver, and keep the speaker volumes at tolerable levels. Now that's a concert I might be inclined to attend.

After a quiet dinner, of course.

Fleming's Prime Steakhouse and Wine Bar in San Diego

## My Beef with Steak Houses

I once considered myself a fan of professional football.
To this day, at the conclusion of every Super Bowl, I ask
the question, "Were I a member of the winning team,
where would I go for the celebration dinner?"

Like football, my little game comes with rules. First,
the restaurant has to be a top-tier steak house. You don't
settle for three here—not after winning a Super Bowl.

Second, the restaurant must be within easy walking
distance of the high-rise condominium my wife and I share
in San Diego's Marina District. Being stuffed like a circus
clown into an Uber Prius, eating my knees as a starter, and
getting whisked to some far-flung outpost is no way to start
a special night out.

Third, the dinner has to commence at a properly
civilized hour—well after 8:00 p.m. This rule applies to all
dinners anywhere, I might add, whether eaten in or out,
and no matter the season. Teresa carries a loaded revolver
in her purse. If ever she catches me eating dinner before
eight, she has specific instructions to shoot me.

As it happens, there are a handful of great steak houses
in close proximity to the Marina District. I'll warn you,
though. If you have to consult the right side of the menu,

*Del Frisco's Double Eagle Steakhouse, San Diego*

you're probably in the wrong place. Fleming's, Morton's, Del Frisco's, Ruth's Chris—these are all personal favorites. In addition to their white linen tablecloths and impeccable service, they share two things in common. Their food is magnificent, and their glittering martinis induce you to laugh at their larceny.

No one steak house is without its shortcomings, however, and that is the keynote of the remainder of this scrappy essay.

None of these restaurants requires men to wear jackets, for example, a policy that would markedly elevate the ambiance of any mahogany walled chophouse. Imagine the horror—you have a starched napkin tucked into your shirt. You're about to take a first bite of precious tartare of Wagyu beef when a crush of barbarians crowds the door, dressed in attire that suggests they've just come from the upper deck at Petco Park—shorts, T-shirts, ball caps, and sandals. But that's San Diego for you. No dress code, anywhere. Imagine the franchise you could build in America's Finest City, renting out blue blazers to restaurants.

Another common flaw is these steak houses don't prepare their Caesar salads tableside, which is the mark of a classy joint. Even the Ranchers Club of New Mexico, in Albuquerque, does a tableside Caesar, and I'm a sucker for it every time. The beauty of a raw egg yolk gliding along the bottom of a vast bowl affords me a visceral pleasure, like watching a sunset. Also, there's a utilitarian aspect to having the Caesar prepared at my elbow—I can supervise the mincing of the anchovies and garlic to ensure sufficient quantities of both. A proper Caesar salad must be lusty.

Another pet peeve: whenever I order a New York steak the way it ought to be prepared—rare—the server's eyes invariably turn up to me, and he says, in question form, "Cool red center?" I bristle. I've reached an age at which I qualify for Medicare. I stand 6′3″ and weigh a hair short of 250 pounds. Do you honestly think I don't know what I'm ordering when I ask for a rare New York steak?

Speaking of pet peeves, I harbor a severe contempt for overflow dining rooms. The shaky chairs, the cramped tables, the panoramas of windowless walls—these banes of fine dining leave me feeling cheated and miserable before the first course. I am not one for making rules, but overflow dining rooms should be outlawed, violations punishable by long prison terms.

I'll never be a member of a team that wins a Super Bowl. However, there's a reason this mother-of-all-celebration dinners has been on my mind. My novel *The Dining Car* recently won an award—a pretty good one, at that. It's an event worth celebrating; I may never win another award. Hell, I may never finish writing another novel.

I've decided my celebration dinner will be held at Fleming's Prime Steakhouse and Wine Bar (380 K Street, San Diego). Its red-leather booths, defensible martinis, and sweet chili calamari all factored into the decision, as did a loyal server named Mike, who's a scratch golfer and can tell you the winemaker and vintage of the glass of red that my brother, Chris, overturned one Sunday night three years ago at one of Mike's tables. Being that it's a special occasion, I'll request a booth at the front, where I can peek through the shutters and keep an eye on the passing trains.

The steaks at Fleming's are consistently cooked to perfection. The restaurant offers several options under the banner "steak companions," one of which is to take your steak Oscar style: garnished with jumbo lump crabmeat and *sauce béarnaise*. I won't go for it. That would be like wearing a frilly shirt and tucking your pant legs into your shiny black boots at a rodeo.

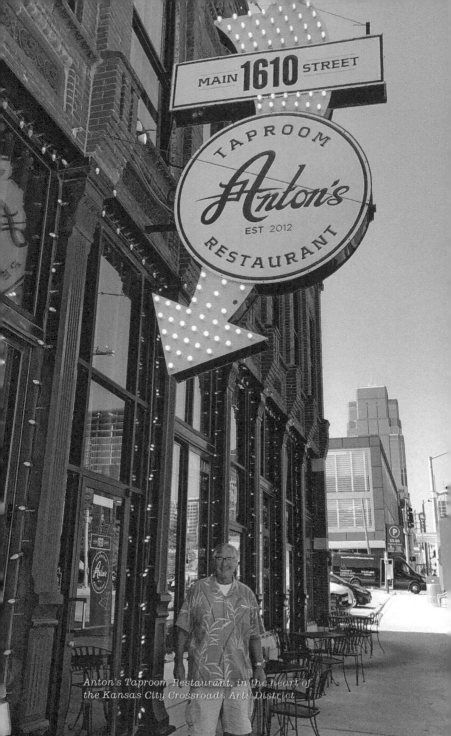

*Anton's Taproom Restaurant, in the heart of
the Kansas City Crossroads Arts District*

## Kansas City Hazards

Kansas City is known for its food, jazz, and a thriving arts scene, but it deserves one black mark of shame. Its airport is one of the worst I've ever seen.

The cramped gates, the unusually large population of the lobotomized shuffling through the constricted terminal, the sluggardly, shamefully disorganized baggage-claim system—it's enough to make a seasoned traveler load up on solid-lead fishing sinker weights and go in search of the nearest mill pond.

As for the frequency of the airport's rental car shuttles and their malicious drivers, I've never seen such foot-dragging. Cattle are treated more expeditiously—and arrive at the slaughterhouse in a better mood.

Another thing about Kansas City: I'm not one to genuflect at the altar of barbecue. Going to Kansas City and having barbecue is like going to the Stanford Library and checking out a Stieg Larsson book. You can do it, but with so many more interesting choices, why would you?

Too many so-called BBQ palaces simply offer inferior cuts of meat, baked beans, french fries, coleslaw, and potato salad—a fare more geared to satisfying the appetites

of a pack of wild dogs than the palates of those with a
semblance of good taste.

And in most barbecue joints, the ambiance matches the
superficial food: sticky floors, dirty tables, long lines. The
kitchens are manned by miscreants who, with their prison
tattoos and covered heads, I suspect are ex-cons on parole.
The drill for ordering food is as undignified as it is inflexible.
With short tempers and menacing scowls, the employees at
the cash registers demand your order in the same tone of
voice with which they might demand, some hours later in a
darkened alley and in the company of their cooks, your Rolex.

Incidentally, certain Southern California barbecue
chains have doubled down on the ignominious, stand-in-
line approach to getting food, making the process even more
undignified for the customer. They issue electronic red
buzzers that, when the eats are ready, trigger off a sequence
of noise, flashing lights, and pulsations that threaten the
customer with electric shock and could quite possibly lead
to convulsions.

This curmudgeon is still trying to calculate the
degree of self-loathing a restaurant patron must harbor to
voluntarily accept a red buzzer from a perfect stranger and
then to stand shoulder-to-shoulder with other suckers in the
lobby of a third-rate restaurant, waiting for his turn to eat,
sometimes for more than an hour. You'd see me dead first.

But back to Kansas City. Lest you think I am anything
but a fan of this Paris of the Plains, let me here and forever
set you straight. My reward for navigating through the
nightmarish airport was Kansas City itself, a remarkably
clean, friendly, all-around welcoming place, where even the
homeless hold doors for ladies who happen to be passing by.

The gentlemen of the grass happily volunteer directions for lost tourists, too—gratuities not included.

Teresa and I eventually got our rental car and checked in to the Sheraton Kansas City at Crown Center, a high-rise hotel in the heart of the city, mere blocks from historic Union Station. Our view of the Kansas City train yards was magnificent.

Soon we were off to dinner. I'm a sucker for old mahogany paneled steak houses, and in the fashionable and upscale Country Club Plaza, a short Uber ride away, there was a celebrated chophouse that has been in operation— and family owned—for four decades. At the Plaza, Teresa and I alighted from our ride. The tree-lined street was surrounded by trendy, open-air restaurants bustling with exhilarated diners. We entered our acclaimed steak house and found it... empty.

It was like being in the presence of a legendary, elderly monarch lying on a bed of woe, clinging to life, while the world outside carries merrily on. The vacant bar, the silent dining room, the skeleton staff holding things together as best they could, the novice server grimly going through the rote of presenting the night's specials—it pointed sadly to the imminent demise of this venerable establishment.

Based on the food, I'd recommend posting a *Do Not Resuscitate* order on the back of the menu.

The oysters Rockefeller was banal and uninspiring. They offered it in servings of four. *Four*? Whoever heard of oysters Rockefeller served in four? My New York steak was puny. It looked like something I might've had forty years ago at Sizzler, while on a high school dinner date. The sautéed spinach was so dry that it constituted a fire hazard.

I won't mention this steak house by name, but you'll read about it soon enough in the obituaries.

It was here in Kansas City, on this very same trip, that I had one of the most memorable meals of my life. Anton's Taproom Restaurant appears to be a hole in the wall. You'll find it at 1610 Main Street, in an unassuming structure in the heart of the Kansas City Crossroads Arts District. At the behest of Jerry, the restaurant's middle-aged, good-humored ambassador-manager who doubled as our server, Teresa and I split a 32-ounce, cut-to-order, dry-aged, grass-fed, antibiotic-free porterhouse steak. It had the texture of sashimi—and was hands down the best, most flavorful beef I have ever tasted.

*Anton's 32-ounce porterhouse steak*

Jerry talked us into the charcuterie starter—a good choice for a restaurant that has a retail meat market on the premises and makes its own salumi, prosciutto, and pork rillettes. At Jerry's urging, we also started with an order of roasted bone marrow. We scooped the bone marrow and residual fat onto pieces of crusty bread. The beef bones, nearly as long and thick as police batons, came with smoked brisket sausage on the side.

This extravagant lunch cost a pretty penny—with daughter Katie, and her husband, Lucas, there were four of us, and the tab exceeded the combined cost of our two hotel rooms for the night, but what's money for, anyway? On our way out the door, Jerry told us about a signature cocktail called the Bone Marrow Luge—a shot of whiskey sucked through the hollow of a beef marrow bone.

Wide-eyed, I looked at Lucas, and Lucas looked at me. There wasn't time; after this long lunch we had a Royals-Indians game to catch, but you can bet we'll beat a path back to Anton's the next time we're in Kansas City.

And for the record, on your trip home, when you queue up for the security line inside the Kansas City airport, don't get behind a guy named Bill. You'll know him when you see him. He wears suspenders over a red plaid shirt and carries a brown Samsonite suitcase secured with a strap, and he's on his way to Lockhart, Texas, to eat barbecue.

Seafood in San Diego.
Isn't the world's deepest, largest ocean just down the block?

# Floundering in an Ocean of Disappointment

Frankly, I'm a meat-and-potatoes guy, but as your ersatz food writer and restaurant critic, it dawned on me that a dispatch on the state of San Diego's seafood restaurants is long overdue.

However, I was tentative about doing the research for this essay. I've always considered fish a waste of a good appetite. But now I realize that going out to a restaurant and ordering a piece of fish is like visiting your crazy Aunt Bessie in the retirement home. You do it overy once in a while because you know it's the right thing to do, and when you finally do it, it isn't nearly as bad as you thought it would be.

In my snooty world, seafood restaurants are segmented like the ecosystem of the ocean, rendered in cutaway fashion on a poster that hung in one of my middle school science classrooms. Dwelling on the muddy floor are lowly sea creatures too numerous to count—the "quick-service restaurants" where you stand at a filthy counter and order from items listed on a menu board. Most everything in this low-end counter category is deep-fried and called a fish taco.

Still deep in the briny restaurant milieu are the low-end sit-down establishments. A high school student masquerading as a restaurant hostess seats you in a brightly lit dining room that has brass portholes instead of windows. The heavily lacquered tables are covered with paper place-mats and an unidentifiable goo. The walls are adorned with rusty sea anchors, fragments of boat parts, and colorful glass floats bound in fishnets. The servers are poorly trained, if at all. These places abound in noise and germs, their laminated menus stick to your hands, everything smells like fish, and you walk out feeling actively ill. You'd find a better wine list in a gas station.

When it comes to seafood restaurants in the fine-dining category, meaning where, in my science poster of bygone days, the ocean meets the sky, the gold standard was Scott's Seafood Grill and Bar in Orange County, California. In 1989, Englishman Malcolm Stroud, a formally trained chef who once plied his trade aboard regal passenger ships in the Cunard Line, teamed up with Simon Snellgrove, an Australian financier, to open this elegant, landmark restaurant amid some of the highest-priced retail properties known to man: South Coast Plaza.

Located adjacent to the Segerstrom Center for the Arts, Scott's Seafood Grill and Bar was a restaurant palace to behold. Its vast and well-appointed dining room buzzed with the energy of an opening night on Broadway. Chic and fashionable theatergoers packed the restaurant's upholstered booths and vast, round tables. The white linen was always fresh, as were the stunning floral arrangements that brightened the classic plantation-style interior. In the wide aisles, busy servers dodged one another, delivering champagne in ice buckets here, oysters on the half shell there. As curtain time at the Arts Center drew near, a busser went through the dining room, sounding a chime.

To this day, the lemon-garlic calamari at Scott's has not been duplicated.

With Scott's in Costa Mesa, Stroud and Snellgrove elevated the gastronomic and sensuous experience of fine dining in a dinner house where the slant was decidedly in favor of seafood, building on white-tablecloth, legendary restaurants like Jake's Famous Crawfish in Portland, Oregon, and the Legal Sea Foods chain on the East Coast.

*Jake's Famous Crawfish, in Portland, OR, has been serving seafood for more than a century*

Scott's Seafood in Costa Mesa closed in 2015 when Snellgrove decided not to renew the lease, and the world has never been the same.

Scott's had its roots in San Francisco. Stroud opened his first restaurant, the Coachman, on Powell Street, in 1961. In 1976, he opened the first Scott's Seafood, at Lombard and Scott, in the Marina District. Stroud went on to hang the Scott's banner on eight restaurants in the Bay Area, Sacramento, and Orange County.

In addition to being an incomparable chef, Mr. Stroud was a gentleman, a golfer, and a perfectionist. He helped several of his employee-chefs open their own restaurants. Few things about fine dining horrified him more than food touching other food on a plate. He passed away in 2012 at the age of 79.

To this day, Mr. Stroud's loss is profoundly felt throughout Southern California's fine-dining seafood landscape. And, unfortunately in San Diego, few restaurants are on par with Scott's. I can't even find one that I would patronize at dinnertime with zeal. I've seen some beautiful, inviting build-outs, perused some promising menus, and chatted with some amiable, well-intended managers, but when the food comes out, the flamboyant promises of the bill of fare prove the emperor's clothes: calamari with the consistency of chalk, Caesar salads so bland they could've originated at a coffee shop, and sea bass so stinky that I could smell it coming out of the kitchen. And far too often, food touching other food with reckless abandon.

I remain shark bitten to explain why quality seafood in Southern California is so spotty. Isn't the world's deepest, largest ocean just down the block?

*In San Diego, the Fish Market is a safe choice for a casual seafood lunch*

Let's revisit the poster. Closer to the surface, where the water is turning blue, we find the crème de la crème of casual-dining seafood restaurants. Better wine lists, heftier cutlery, fresh fish, a trained and knowledgeable waitstaff— in San Diego, I put the Fish Market, at 750 N. Harbor Drive, at the top of the casual-dining category.

The Fish Market's ample menu and unobstructed view of the bay make it a winning choice for a rainy day lunch, when the crowds are down. Their cioppino is perhaps the best I've had anywhere, not counting my table at home, when Teresa is doing the cooking.

If, like me, you have a compulsion for tearing off chunks of toasted sourdough French bread and shamelessly

*Sally's at the Manchester Grand Hyatt is perhaps the best people-watching spot in San Diego*

mopping up the stew in your cioppino bowl, ask for a paper bib along with your crab and lobster tools, and wear it proudly. It signifies that you're one of us.

An equally inspired choice for lunch is Sally's Fish House & Bar, at the Manchester Grand Hyatt (1 Market Pl.). Its delightful, sun-drenched patio overlooking the Marriott Marina is perhaps the best people-watching spot in town, and their selection of entrée salads will satisfy even the most health-conscious diner. The Baja Cobb is a work of art. The fish and chips, made from sea bass and served with steak fries and malt vinegar, is borderline decadent.

For larger appetites, try the open-faced blackened swordfish sandwich or the grilled beef burger, which may be the best hamburger south of The Veranda Fireside Lounge & Restaurant at the Rancho Bernardo Inn.

Fortunately, where dinner is concerned, the dearth in higher-end seafood restaurants comes with an elegant workaround. Fish lovers can get the best of Poseidon's crop at a handful of reputable downtown steak houses: Del Frisco's Double Eagle Steak House, Ruth's Chris, Fleming's, and Morton's. Pan-seared halibut, sesame-crusted ahi tuna, miso-glazed Chilean sea bass, Alaskan king crab legs, whole baked Maine lobsters, chilled seafood towers and sweet chili calamari to start—the broad array of seafood options clicks nicely with the sumptuous steaks, liberal martinis, and lavish wine lists that keep me counting myself a happy regular of these watering holes.

But this doesn't mean I've given up entirely on seafood in San Diego.

If, at dinnertime, you're out in the Gaslamp District and you spot an old chap in deerstalker fore-and-aft cap, Inverness cape, and smoking a calabash pipe, leave him alone. It's Sherlock Holmes. I've commissioned him to find one decent fine-dining seafood restaurant in San Diego.

Last I heard, he's still looking.

# Getting By

Rescue 93 commands its share of attention,
particularly when stocking up at the liquor store

## My Fire Truck

My wife, Teresa, takes first prize for the best gift ever. She bought me a fire truck.

The truck, a red 1987 Ford F-350 crew cab pickup named *Rescue 93*, commands more than its share of attention, particularly when it's parked in front of a liquor store and I'm stocking up on cases of wine, Jack Daniel's Tennessee Sour Mash Whiskey, and Tito's Handmade Vodka.

As I load booze into the fire truck, I like to wink at old ladies and tell them the boys and girls at the station need to blow off a little steam.

One of the truck's many charms is that it's steeped in a history of firehouse scandal.

*Rescue 93* went to auction a few years back when the disgraced San Pasqual Volunteer Fire Department, near my home in northern San Diego County, was given the death penalty by the County Board of Supervisors.

The volunteer fire department's capital crime: water theft.

Tom Carter, a Poway, California, resident and owner of a palatial hilltop home, was waiting to get his property connected to the city's metered water line. In the meantime, he relied on well water.

*I can park anywhere—meter maids ignore it*

At the time, Southern California was experiencing a major drought. Mr. Carter's well was going dry, and his extensive landscaping was in danger of dying.

Mr. Carter asked Charles Dilts, a church friend and vice president of the San Pasqual Volunteer Fire Department's board of directors, to step in and help.

According to news reports, Mr. Dilts directed San Pasqual Fire Chief Chris Kisslinger to send the department's 2,500-gallon water tender to Carter's property, where the homeowner had the tank capacity to store up to 10,000 gallons.

On four separate occasions, San Pasqual's tender serviced Mr. Carter's water tanks by filling up at a Poway city fire hydrant, then emptying the water into Mr. Carter's tanks.

Helping out a church friend, don't you know?

The Robin Hood-in-reverse scheme constituted the theft of thousands of gallons of unmetered water from the city of Poway. A town loyalist noticed the interloping fire truck filling up at the hydrant, snapped a photo, and reported the culpable water rustlers to authorities.

It was a bad day for the rural volunteer fire department, which maintained its station in the heart of the San Pasqual Valley, off Academy Road.

"I'm sorry to say, there is a history of bad choices at the San Pasqual Volunteer Fire Department," said San Diego County Supervisor Bill Horn in a written statement. "Enough is enough."

Poway levied a $1,000 fine, the San Diego County Sheriff's Department opened a criminal investigation, and the San Diego Board of Supervisors set in motion the volunteer fire department's dissolution.

Though *Rescue 93* was for all intents and purposes an innocent bystander in the water theft, the stalwart truck was banished to the ignominy of civilian life when Cal Fire assumed control of the department and moved its own equipment into the station. (*Rescue 93*'s final service call, according to the log still in the cab, was for a medical-assist.)

After being sold at auction, *Rescue 93* fell into my wife's hands as the perfect gift for the man who has (almost) everything.

Under my superintendence, the comedown for *Rescue 93* continued: I repurposed the truck from the fire department to the sanitation department. On a weekly basis it now ferries our trash barrels to the bottom of our long driveway, where the colossal beasts of EDCO, a family-

*Reassigned to the sanitation department*

owned waste collection and recycling company, take the barrels overhead on robotic king crab's legs and shake them like salt and pepper shakers.

When *Rescue 93*'s truck bed is free of trash barrels, it still makes for a convincing fire truck. A more appropriate name for the truck would be "Stolen Valor." Wherever I take it, police officers wave, firemen wave, and women swoon.

Better yet, meter maids ignore it. I can park anywhere I want to.

My biggest fear of taking the truck out is that I'll come across a nasty street accident. Rather than shrug at the carnage and gore—I'm no paramedic or firefighter—I've rehearsed the perfect response to that citizen who flags me down: "You think this accident's bad, you ought to see the one I'm going to!"

I must warn you. There's a downside to owning a fire truck. You'll want to acquire more. The impulse to buy gets into your blood, like collecting diesel locomotives, old cabooses, and private railroad cars.

Though I haven't told Teresa, I've already started looking for my next fire truck. I found a vintage 1966 Seagraves fire truck that's for sale—good tires, brakes and horns work, the windshield is cracked. This truck has steel steps going up to the hose bed, which has been modified with benches and seat belts. The listing says the truck can be used for parades and kiddies' birthday parties, but I'm thinking I'll take it downtown and run booze cruises for conventioneers and Shriners.

On another website, I found a 2003 Pierce custom pumper fire truck—the real thing—for $45,995. This one, I could just drive around. How tempting is that?

But then again, this is how bad museums get started. I can already hear my grandchildren after I pass: "But Grammie, you can't sell Grampy's fire trucks!"

I won't do this to Teresa, I keep telling myself. But then again, I might.

As the holiday season rolls around, if you're shopping for someone who has everything, consider getting them a fire truck.

You can't go wrong.

Siemens Mobility's SC-44 Charger locomotives are built in California

## Amtrak's New Clothes

Have you seen Amtrak's new diesel-electric locomotives?

They're built by Siemens Mobility, a division of Siemens, the global German conglomerate. They look like sausages.

When I saw one of these engines parked at San Diego's Santa Fe Depot, the name "Siemens" painted on the side, my first thought was, "What bonehead at Amtrak just bought a fleet of locomotives from Germany?"

I was hasty in my criticism.

Siemens Mobility's SC-44 Charger locomotives are built just south of Sacramento at the company's French Road factory, a 600,000 square-foot facility on a 60-acre campus. The factory employs more than 1,300 workers.

The 4,400 horsepower, 16-cylinder Cummins QSK95 diesel engines that power these locomotives are manufactured in Seymour, Indiana.

The Seymour-Sacramento collaboration makes the Charger locomotive "Buy American" compliant, according to Amtrak.

Amtrak ordered seventy-five of these sausage-shaped locomotives to replace its aging locomotive fleet. The order was valued at $850 million and will be funded "from the railway's own resources," Amtrak says. In addition to

*Amtrak engines look more and more like hot dogs these days*

supplying the locomotives, Siemens will provide parts and
technical support for twenty years.

Siemens remains tight-lipped about any obligation
to supply twenty years of mustard, hot dog buns, or pickle
relish for their sausages.

It takes about forty-five days to build a Charger
locomotive, and the company can make four at a time,
Siemens says.

Amtrak will take delivery of the locomotives between
2021 and 2024. The railroad plans to put the new engines

into service principally on their long-distance trains, including the *California Zephyr*, the *Coast Starlight*, and the *Southwest Chief*. (At present, the majority of Amtrak's long-distance trains are powered by General Electric P42DC Genesis Series 1 locomotives, which look more like serpents than sausages. If you know anyone who has a horror story about their Amtrak train breaking down, leaving passengers stranded for hours, it likely involved a P-42 locomotive.)

*Amtrak's P-42 Genesis engines, a '90s-era locomotive, look more like serpents than sausages*

*A Santa Fe F7, a '50s-era locomotive, in famous Warbonnet paint scheme, Galveston Railroad Museum*

State-supported Amtrak routes, such as the *Pacific Surfliner*, in California, and the *Amtrak Cascades*, in Washington, have already pressed these SC-44 Charger locomotives into service. Washington's Charger locomotive #1402 led the inaugural run of *Cascades* Train #501, which derailed in December 2017 as it approached a bridge over I-5 near Lakewood, Washington. Three people died in the accident, and several automobiles on the freeway were crushed.

The data recorder showed the train was traveling at seventy-eight miles an hour, nearly fifty miles an hour over the train's speed limit for that section of track.

*An Amtrak P-42 departs Tucson*

Ironically, speed is one advantage these Charger locomotives have over the locomotives they'll replace. They can
operate at up to 125 miles an hour, compared to a top speed
of 90–100 miles an hour for the P-42.

There are other advantages to the Siemens locomotives:
more hauling power, increased reliability, less noise, lower
emissions, and improved safety features, such as Positive
Train Control, which was not in effect at the time of the
Lakewood *Cascades* crash.

The prospect of a diesel-electric sausage pulling a
classic train like the *Southwest Chief* saddens me. It signals
the end of an era in American railroading.

Give me old fashioned multi-chime horns sounding in
the distance, a Mars light oscillating on the nose of an elegant
EMD F7 streamliner, the thrum of its power plant reverber-
ating through your bones as the locomotive passes, soot and
smoke belching from its roof exhaust, the train running
sixteen hours late—this to me will always be true railroading.

Alfred Hitchcock's classic movie *North by Northwest* ends with an iconic scene. The year is 1959. Cary Grant is on a train, in a sleeper car's double bedroom, squeezed into the upper berth. "Come along, Mrs. Thornhill," he says as he pulls damsel-in-distress Eva Marie Saint up onto the narrow bed beside him. Cut to a nighttime shot of two Southern Pacific F7 diesel locomotives hauling a train of fluted streamliner cars into a tunnel. Roll credits.

Now I ask you this: Who wants to see Cary Grant and Eva Marie Saint climbing into an upper berth on a German-built, sausage-like, diesel-electric train with Tier-4 emissions technology that runs on time?

Less noise, crazy fast speeds, the promise of more reliable engines—it makes you wonder what this world is coming to.

Mother Nature serves as a sanctuary to all things human

## Respite from the Backside Slide of Literary Society

The disappearance of sanatoriums, like the decline of rudimentary English grammar skills and formal evening dress on cruise ships, serves as further proof of a society on a downhill slide.

Butterflies flitting in sun-drenched gardens; fountains burbling on a spacious piazza; nurses in starched white uniforms pouring tea—the sanatorium once served as sanctuary to anyone of means in need of a respite from a condition I'll call *desponderant animos*—exasperation with all things human.

My time of want for a mountaintop sanctuary came a few weeks back, when a ribald, lollapalooza of a street orgy invaded my clean, quiet city. I should have known it was coming. Comic-Con comes to San Diego every summer.

On a lark, thinking I might learn something about several generations of media consumers who've made *LEGO Batman* a top performer at the box office and *Harry Potter* a billion-dollar book franchise, I set out for a walk among these enthusiastic convention goers.

The people and things I encountered on the streets of San Diego were less than reassuring, if not downright alarming. Fat, bearded men carried swords, shields, and ray guns while gobbling Subway sandwiches. Buxom women in bustiers, corsets, and fishnet stockings struck provocative poses for amateur photographers. And everywhere you looked there were impersonators of Superman, Superwoman, Spiderman, and Darth Vader; bald pates and potbellies; bare midriffs and eye patches; bloody knives, bloody spears, and bloody chainsaws. Though I can't tell you what a druid is, I'm pretty sure I passed several.

Even the buses circulating the perimeter of the gridlock got in on the game. They sported gruesome wraps promising zombies, bloodletting, and intergalactic warfare to come.

As a writer of literary fiction, the spectacle of Comic-Con hit me particularly hard. In my novels *The Dining Car* and *Sunshine Chief*, my characters engage in conversation rather than interplanetary warfare. They travel in vintage private railroad cars and not aboard hurtling spaceships. They eat oysters Rockefeller and herb-crusted, roasted rack of lamb as opposed to human flesh, and their petty conflicts involve status, power, and acceptance rather than saving planet Earth. I write books I can't even give away. Meanwhile Comic-Con routinely outdraws the Super Bowl.

To put it in perspective the Port of San Diego, landlord and crowned head of San Diego's waterfront, is actively pursuing proposals to expand its convention center for the express purpose of accommodating the ever-growing Comic-Con crowds. Meanwhile, in the Port District's own Seaport Village, San Diego's last downtown bookseller, Upstart Crow Bookstore & Coffeehouse, recently shuttered its doors.

Feeling extremely sorry for myself—out of fashion as a writer, hopelessly out of step in my chosen literary genre—and to silence the howling in my ears, I dashed into a corner liquor store for a fifth of Johnnie Walker Black, flagged down a private ambulance, and directed the EMT at the wheel to deliver me to the nearest thing I knew to a modern sanatorium: The Ritz-Carlton, Lake Tahoe.

*Enjoying the cool, clear waters of Lake Tahoe*

One of North America's premier mountain resorts,
The Ritz-Carlton sits perched like a Bavarian castle on the
vertical slopes above the town of Truckee, California, which
in winter registers some of the lowest temperature readings
in the lower 48 states.

In summer, the views from the giant picture
windows are of green meadows, sheer, bare ski runs, and
fog-shrouded forests in the valleys below. At twilight, as you
stand in the tastefully decorated great room of this exalted
hotel, a martini in hand, a roaring fire at your back, and as
you contemplate the dramatic, snowcapped mountain peak
just beyond the expansive outdoor deck, you half expect to
spot Captain Georg von Trapp and his bratty brood of seven
meandering up a trail to the summit ahead, fleeing not
Georg's commission in the Third Reich's navy but a series
of unpaid Reno bar tabs.

You'll find the guest rooms in this luxurious resort
worthy of the Ritz-Carlton brand—spacious, attractively
furnished, and clean. The in-room TVs are big and the
glittering bathrooms are exquisite.

The onsite restaurant, Manzanita, with its open kitchen
and natural materials of wood, stone, and glass, is as
breathtaking as it is welcoming. The items on the dinner
menu will pamper your sense of taste throughout your stay.
Start with the lobster bisque, and when you're looking for
an alternative to the Durham Ranch prime filet mignon,
try the short ribs with morel mushroom and bone marrow,
or the Niman Ranch pork tomahawk chop.

Breakfast always tastes better in the mountains. Tame
your hangover with a classic eggs Benedict or a fulfilling
huevos rancheros. And upon your return from Truckee,

where you've spent the morning in a lawn chair, watching a long line of freight trains descending from Donner Pass, I suggest a late lunch of chicken pappardelle, a Manzanita burger, or a salmon BLT (Applewood bacon and heirloom tomato with Bibb lettuce on a brioche bun).

More than food, wine, and trains, this mountain resort is about serenity and quiet, about taking time to ponder life and life's choices—in other words, a sanatorium boasting the modern conveniences of a world-class hotel.

Gazing out the floor-to-ceiling windows, thinking about the crowds of Comic-Con and my journey as a writer, I decided to forgo the traditional writerly handwringing about staying true to my craft and not taking the hemlock of writing for the mass market. A voice chanted in my head: "If you can't beat 'em, join 'em... join 'em... join 'em...."

The plot for my new science fiction novel is this: Aliens invade Earth. Studying California, the chief alien, who has a degree in anthropology, concludes that Caltrans workers, in their fluorescent orange vests and hardhats, are the high priests of society, and that the endless lines of cars that snake past them on the state's crumbling freeways are in fact parades in reverse—human beings who come from miles around to pay homage to their exalted leaders. (This alien anthropologist has a high-functioning insect brain and doesn't always get everything 100% right.)

Assuming human form and dressed in Caltrans garb, the aliens descend on Sacramento, where they demand concessions from a legion of smarmy politicians. The governor misconstrues the aliens for a bargaining unit of the International Union of Operating Engineers, Caltrans's largest union, and quickly accedes to their demands.

He hands over the keys to planet Earth, and mankind is soon annihilated.

The manuscript has some rough spots, I'll grant you, but I'm in the process of smoothing these out.

Publishing houses and literary agents can reach me through my website. The TV and movie rights remain available.

Museum
Is Open

The museum is now open to the public

## Museum of the Unknown Writer

The Eric Peterson Home and Museum touts itself as one of the top destination tourist attractions in Southern California. With its high arched windows, terra-cotta colonnades, whitewashed walls, and red tile roof, the two-story manor, which sits on a hill above the San Pasqual Valley, in northern San Diego County, serves as a textbook example of Spanish Colonial Revival architecture.

Eric Peterson, the novelist, still lives and writes here, having called it home for nearly fifteen years. Inspired by the Ernest Hemingway Home and Museum in Key West, Florida, and by the Steinbeck House Restaurant and Museum in Salinas, California, Peterson and his wife, Teresa, opened their home to the public in 2018.

"The artist's house as museum solves the predicament of the unknown writer struggling to make ends meet on his book royalties alone," Peterson explains in a video that loops in the sunny high-ceilinged foyer, which doubles as the museum's reception area. "Hemingway and Steinbeck both made a tactical error in opening their museums posthumously. I say, Why wait till you're dead?"

We found the museum easy to get to. The parking was accessible, though somewhat pricey ($17). On the morning

*Parking was both pricey and plentiful*

we arrived, we noticed ours was the only car in the parking lot, which consisted entirely of dirt.

We hiked up a steep driveway to the house, where yet again we were separated from our money. Adult admission was $13; children under eighteen were $9. Children under twelve, the sign said, "were not welcome at any price."

*Jagged, irregular walkways threatened to twist our ankles,*
*rendering us hobbled and gimpy for the guided tour*

Our visit began with a walk around the house.
Expecting to see exquisite gardens, exotic trees, and
sweeping views of the valley, we found instead old
lawnmowers, chipped concrete fountains, and sprinkler
lines leaking water like blood. The crabgrass abounded with
fresh gopher mounds. The swimming pool was green from
neglect. Jagged, irregular walkways threatened to twist our
ankles, rendering us hobbled and gimpy for the guided tour.

*Grail space—the writer's desk*

On the museum's website, unnamed recent visitors recommended the guided tour. This tour promises a behind-the-scenes look at the historic manuscripts, modern sculptures, desert landscape paintings, and workspaces that inspired Peterson through his most prolific writing period, culminating in his masterpiece novel *The Dining Car* (Huckleberry House, 341 pages, $26.95/$16.95), for which he won the Benjamin Franklin Gold Award for Popular Fiction.

At 6'3" and weighing nearly 250 pounds, our tour guide could have been the author himself but for his long beard and black sunglasses, which he refused to take off. (Peterson is known to be clean shaven.) As luck would have it, we'd missed the actual writer by minutes. He was away either to get paper or ink toner for his printer—we never quite got the story straight.

Peterson's lack of productivity—he's written only two novels in ten years—is a recognized testament to his lethargy behind the keyboard. But is there more to the story?

We think so. It's one of the reasons we visited the house.

The clean, airy kitchen was most notable for its hidden bar. Concealed in two large pullout drawers were some thirty bottles of top-shelf spirits, liqueurs, and mixers. A plethora of martini glasses and silver shakers adorned the glass shelves. A padlocked Sub-Zero wine chiller appeared amply stocked.

"Could a fondness for bottle waving be responsible for Peterson's overpowering lassitude?" we wondered.

We posed the question to our tour guide. He bristled, and the color rose in his cheeks. He turned on his heels and led us to the south end of the house.

Peterson's library, a big room, shocked us nearly speechless. We hadn't seen so many mindless, lowbrow books all in one place since our tour of the Reagan Ranch. There were autobiographies of George Stephanopoulos, Ari Fleischer, and Lee Iacocca. The novels ranged from Erich Segal's *Love Story* to a Nicholas Sparks literary meltdown too gruesome to name. The only thing missing to make this a provincial trifecta for dolts was a condensed books anthology from Reader's Digest.

*The bookcase in the upstairs study*

"You must be kidding," we said to our tour guide. "The vigorous intellectual tour de force behind *Life as a Sandwich* and *The Dining Car* reads this claptrap?"

"It's filler," our guide snapped. "Upstairs in the study— that's where you'll find his true intellectual sustenance."

And boy did we ever. The bookshelves in Peterson's upstairs study were bursting with literary classics like Dan Jenkins's *Semi-Tough*, Larry McMurtry's *Texasville*, Tom Wolfe's *A Man in Full*, and, of course, David Foster Wallace's *The Pale King*.

On one of these same bookshelves, in a white box, we found the original manuscript for *The Dining Car*. In the hands of an irrational, hard-nosed editor, its 110,000 words would be cut to fewer than 80,000.

Peterson writes about—and purports to be—a fastidious gourmet, but we're certain he's no regular of the museum's on-site café, located in the house's three-car garage, which smells of gasoline and mothballs. The prepared food on display inside the curved glass refrigerated display case looked appallingly inedible. Crockpot beans, a raspberry-Jello salad, a chicken and rice casserole, a tuna and noodles potluck casserole—it all seemed to have come directly from your grandmother's funeral reception.

Peterson's museum charges $14 for all you can load onto a single paper plate—the honor system. We took two Cuban sandwiches and put our money in a jar.

We ate sitting at a card table in the garage. A creepy Donald Trump piñata, said to be a gift from Eric Peterson's brother, Chris, who was severely inebriated at the time of the purchase, looked over our shoulders as we ate. As the story goes, the vendor told Chris they were sold out of Hillary Clinton piñatas, which tended to go like hotcakes.

With his lame food, hyperbolic marketing prose, exorbitant prices, and jaw-dropping dearth of engaging exhibits, it's easy to conclude that Peterson, in turning his home into a museum, has shown a palpable disdain for

*The garage does double duty as museum cafeteria*

the readers who are his biggest fans—as if it's their fault he can't sell enough books to make a living.

Yes, bookstores are declining, and readers today are distracted by competing forms of entertainment like social media and Netflix. But we say if he can't cut it as a real writer, maybe it's time for Mr. Peterson to hang it up and find a new line of work.

The museum is open Tuesday through Saturday from 10 a.m. to 5:00 p.m. No reservations are required. All major credit cards accepted.

*The two-story house in northern San Diego County*

## About the Author

Eric Peterson's debut novel, *Life as a Sandwich*, was a
finalist in the San Diego Book Awards. His second novel,
*The Dining Car*, won the IBPA Benjamin Franklin Gold
Award for Popular Fiction, the San Diego Book Award
Gold Medal for Contemporary Fiction, and the Readers'
Favorite Book Award Silver Medal for Literary Fiction.
*Publishers Weekly*'s Booklife named *The Dining Car* a
"Book to Watch."

Peterson's third novel, *Sunshine Chief*, a sequel to
*The Dining Car*, won the IBPA Benjamin Franklin Silver
Award for General Fiction and was a finalist in the
literary fiction category of the Readers' Favorite Book
Awards. *Museum of the Unknown Writer* is Peterson's
first published collection of essays.

A third-generation Californian, Peterson attended
the University of California at San Diego. He completed
his Communication degree at Stanford, majoring in
journalism. He lives in Southern California with his
wife, Teresa.

ericpetersonauthor.com

Made in the USA
Las Vegas, NV
06 June 2023

73054612R00098